In the Next Volume

During the final, chaotic days of the Meiji Restoration, Kenshin became very well acquainted with the Shinsengumi, an elite troop of formidable swordsmen who policed the streets of Kyoto. Saitō Hajime, once a captain in the Shinsengumi, now appears at the Kamiya Dojo as a member of the Tokyo police force under the name "Fujita Gorō," but has he come to settle old scores or to reawaken Kenshin to his true potential?

Then, the assassination of a prominent member of the Meiji Government forces Kenshin to leave Tokyo on a long journey to Kyoto, Japan's ancient capital. Awaiting him at his goal is the diabolical Shishio Makoto, the hitokiri who replaced Kenshin when he renounced the taking of human life. With a fiendish master plot to irrevocably alter the fate of Japan, Shishio and his fearsome cabal of fighters are prepared to annihilate whoever stands in their path. Will Kenshin be able to remain the gentle "rurouni" with a life-or-death duel looming on the horizon?!

Volume 3 Available Now

Rurouni Kenshin

STORY & ART BY
Nobuhiro Watsuki

Rurouni Kenshin

Volume 2
VIZBIG Edition

STORY AND ART BY
NOBUHIRO WATSUKI

ENGLISH ADAPTATION Gerard Jones
TRANSLATION Kenichiro Yagi
TOUCH-UP ART & LETTERING Steve Dutro
SHONEN JUMP SERIES DESIGN Sean Lee
VIZBIG EDITION DESIGN Courtney Utt
SHONEN JUMP SERIES EDITOR Kit Fox
VIZBIG EDITION EDITORS Leyla Aker & Kit Fox

PRINTED IN CHINA

PUBLISHED BY VIZ MEDIA, LLC
P.O. BOX 77010
SAN FRANCISCO, CA 94107

10 9 8 7 6 5 4 3
FIRST PRINTING, APRIL 2008
THIRD PRINTING, DECEMBER 2015

PARENTAL ADVISORY
RUROUNI KENSHIN is rated T+ for Older Teen and is recommended for ages 16 and up. This volume contains realistic violence, language and alcohol/tobacco usage.
ratings.viz.com

Meiji Swordsman Romantic Story

VOLUME 4
Dual Conclusions

VOLUME 5
The State of Meiji Swordsmanship

VOLUME 6
No Worries

STORY & ART BY
Nobuhiro Watsuki

SHONEN JUMP MANGA · VIZBIG EDITION

Contents

Cast of Characters

Kamiya Kaoru
Acting master of the Kamiya Kasshin-Ryū sword arts dojo left to her by her father.

Himura Kenshin
(Hitokiri Battōsai)
Former assassin for the Ishin Shinshi, or "patriot" faction, now a wandering swordsman.

Myōjin Yahiko
Orphaned from a samurai family, now a member of Team Kenshin.

Sagara Sanosuke
(Zanza)
A fighter for hire and ex-member of the doomed Sekihō Army.

Takani Megumi
Daughter of one of Japan's most prominent medical families.

Sanjō Tsubame
Though she now works at Akabeko, her family has served the Nagaokas for 300 years.

Takeda Kanryū
A young industrialist who has amassed daunting amounts of wealth and power.

Shinomori Aoshi
Head of Kanryū's private army, and former head of Edo Castle's *onmitsu*, or ninja, guard.

Nagaoka Mikio
Son of the prominent Nagaoka family, now a dishonorable thief.

Isurugi Raijūta
With his devastating Shinko-ryū style, he hopes to revitalize swordsmanship in Japan.

Tsukayama Yutarō
An impressionable young boy who idolizes Raijūta and considers himself his disciple.

Tsukioka Tsunan
Former cadet in the Sekihō Army, now surviving as an artist.

Rurouni Kenshin

VOLUME 4: Dual Conclusions

I AM HAN'NYA, MASTER OF INTELLIGENCE OF THE EDO CASTLE ONIWABANSHŪ.
Act 23
The Martial Artist and the Spy
BY ORDER OF THE *OKASHIRA*, I WILL DEFEND THIS SPOT TO THE DEATH!

SUCH STRUGGLE IS UNNECESSARY.
WON'T YOU LET US PASS?
TP
TP
COMMANDS OF THE OKASHIRA
...ARE ABSOLUTE.

!!

METAL... GAUNTLETS BENEATH HIS LEATHER GLOVES.

THAT'S HOW HE STOPPED KENSHIN'S STRIKE THE OTHER NIGHT!

READ THIS WAY
THE GAUNTLETS HELP ABSORB IMPACT, TRUE ENOUGH.
BUT MOSTLY IT WAS HIS *SKILL* AS A MARTIAL ARTIST.
A FIGHT...
...SEEMS INEVITABLE.
YET AGAINST SUCH SKILL...
THIS ONE *CANNOT* HOLD BACK.
THE SAME TO YOU.
LET'S GO.

KIEHHH!
!

DIRECT HIT?!

KNH.

REVERSE STRIKE!

CRUSH !!
BOK

ZZZ

TCH!

YOU FOOL!
ROCKET
KICK!
ORO ?!

WHAT ARE YOU GETTING ALL BEAT UP FOR?!

HURRY AND USE YOUR HITEN MITSURUGI-RYŪ!

THAT WAS THE IDEA...!

HIS PUNCHES, HIS REVERSE STRIKE ...
...DODGED BY A PAPER'S WIDTH!

HOOOOOOO
BUT AT THE LAST MOMENT...
...HIS ARMS STRETCHED!

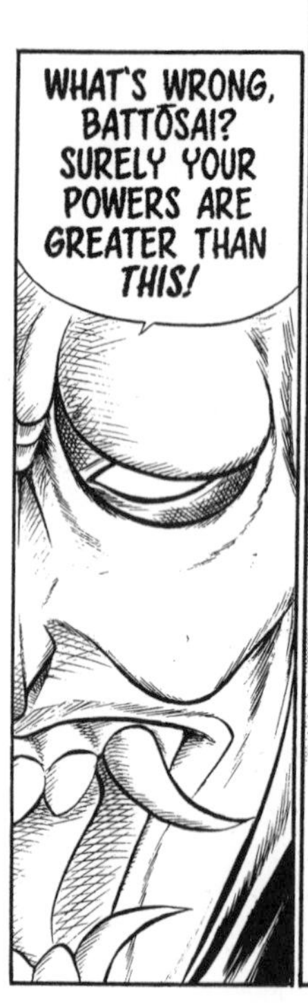

WHAT'S WRONG, BATTŌSAI? SURELY YOUR POWERS ARE GREATER THAN *THIS!*

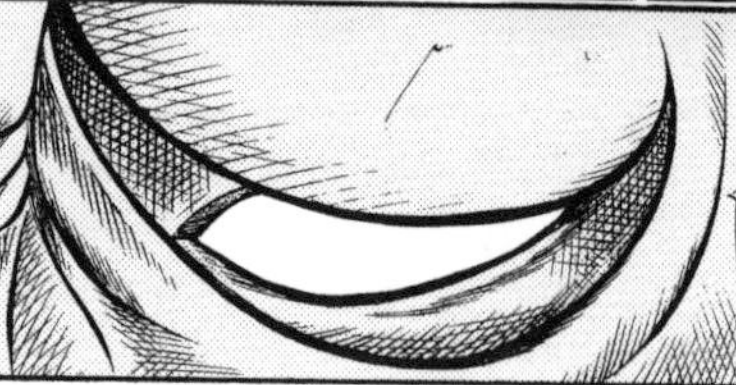

IF YOU CAN'T EVEN BREAK *MY* SPELL...
...YOU WON'T LAST A *MINUTE* AGAINST THE OKASHIRA.

SPELL ?!

I AM HAN'NYA OF THE EDO CASTLE ONI-WABANSHŪ.
I AM A MARTIAL ARTIST, BUT ALSO AN *ONMITSU.* A SPY.

READ THIS WAY

A WEEK AGO, WHEN YOU FIRST SET EYES ON ME...
YOU BEGAN TO FALL UNDER MY SPELL.
YOU HAD NO IDEA.

THEY'VE BEGUN, IT SEEMS.
HAN'NYA IS TOUGH.
IF HIS COMBAT SKILLS ARE NOT ENOUGH... HIS UNDEFEATABLE "ARM-EXTENSION SPELL" *SHOULD* BE.
HIS OPPONENTS HAVE NO CHANCE UNLESS THEY CAN SEE THROUGH THE TRICK.

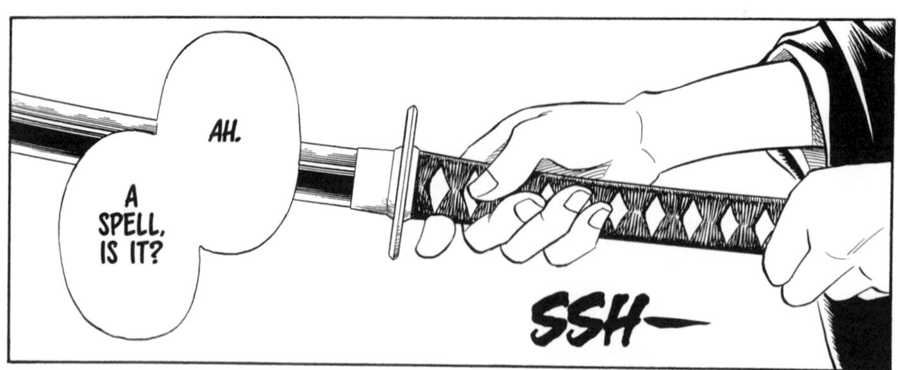

ZAH

ANNOYING, YET...

...EASILY BROKEN!

!

HEY, LITTLE SWORDSMAN—WHAT'S THAT STANCE?
HOW SHOULD I KNOW? NEVER SEEN IT.
PAT
OF THE FIVE BASIC FORMS,* IT'S CLOSEST TO SEIGAN.
THOUGH IT'S CLEARLY NOT SEIGAN...
HANDS OFF THE HEAD.

*BASIC FORMS: JŌDAN, CHŪDAN (SEIGAN), GEDAN, HASSŌ, WAKIGAMAE [SEE GLOSSARY-ED.]

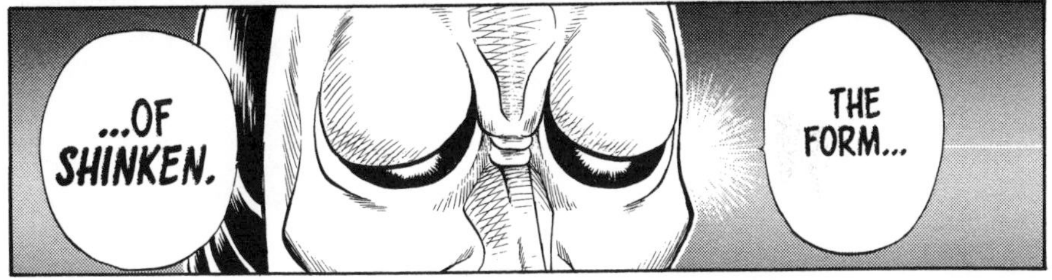
THE FORM...
...OF SHINKEN.

THE ARM EXTENDED HIGHER THAN IN SEIGAN, THE SWORD PARALLEL TO THE GROUND AND POINTING AT THE OPPONENT'S FOREHEAD.
A DEFENSIVE STANCE SEEN IN ANCIENT FIGHTING STYLES, ALLOWING ONE TO REACT INSTANTLY TO ANY SUDDEN CHANGES IN THE OPPONENT'S STRIKES.

GNG
BUT!!

AS A DEFENSIVE FORM, IT MAKES THE TRANSITION TO *OFFENSE* DIFFICULT!!

HYAH!

DON'T TELL ME YOU SHRINK FROM *THIS* FIGHT?!

......

ANSWER ME!!

—......

IS *THIS* THE TRUE FACE...

...OF THE LEGENDARY *HITOKIRI*?!

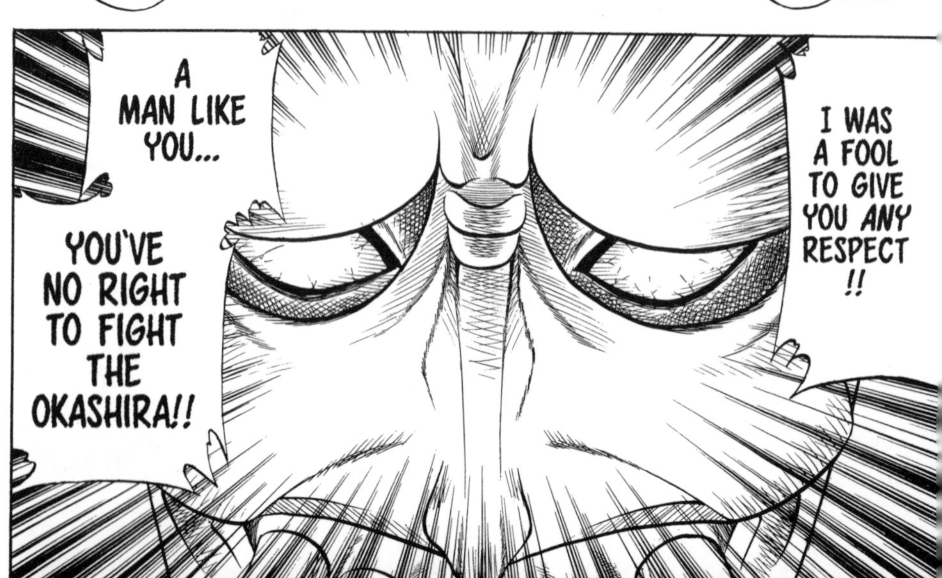

I WAS A FOOL TO GIVE YOU ANY RESPECT!!
A MAN LIKE YOU...
YOU'VE NO RIGHT TO FIGHT THE OKASHIRA!!

YOU DIE...
...WHERE YOU STAND!!
!
NO MATTER HOW STRONG A DEFENSE "SHINKEN" IS...
...YOU'LL NEVER DODGE THIS.
NOT UNLESS YOU CAN SEE *HOW* MY ARMS EXTEND!!

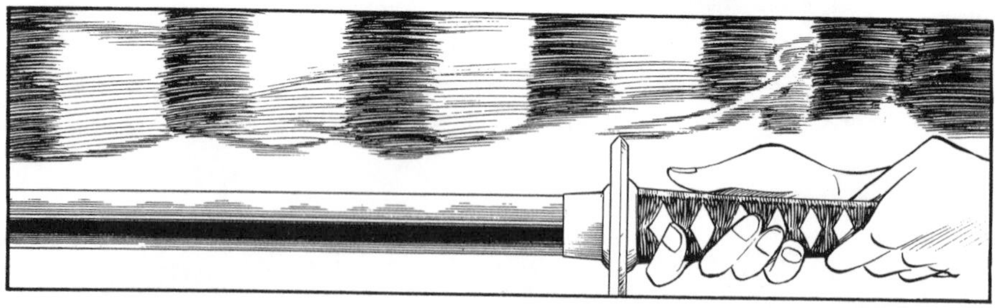

!!!
HEY! HE...
NO MORE SPELL ??

A...
A...
G...
AH...?!
HE DID IT!!

YOU FIGURED IT OUT?

UH-HUH.

IT'S NO MORE THAN...

...THE SIDEWAYS STRIPES TATTOOED ON HIS ARMS.

SIDEWAYS STRIPES...?

OH!

I GET IT! AN *OPTICAL ILLUSION!!*

STRIPES MAKE *ANYTHING* LOOK SHORTER AND WIDER.

THAT'S WHY YOU MISJUDGED HIS REACH!!

HIS REACH WAS A GOOD INCH LONGER THAN I FIRST ESTIMATED...

AND *THAT* DIFFERENCE MADE IT SEEM AS IF HIS ARMS HAD *STRETCHED.*

MEANING, HE COULD LAND A DIRECT HIT AT THE MOMENT OF DODGING.

SO... THEN...

YOUR SHINKEN WAS NOT *ONLY* DEFENSE!!

YOU HELD THE SWORD PARALLEL TO THE GROUND TO MEASURE THE DIFFERENCE BETWEEN PERCEPTION AND THE *REAL* DISTANCE!

SURELY THAT OUTFIT WAS THE FIRST HINT.

A SPY WITH BOLD, GAUDY STRIPES ON BOTH ARMS? UNLIKELY.

THOUGH NO DOUBT THEY'VE HELPED YOU AS A FIGHTER.

AND THEN, OF COURSE, YOU HIDE YOUR EYES WITH THAT MASK, MAKING YOU MORE DIFFICULT TO READ.

STRANGE INDEED, AT FIRST GLANCE—BUT IN FACT A PERFECTLY CONCEIVED BATTLE COSTUME!

READ THIS WAY

THAT WOULD ALL BE TRUE.
EXCEPT THAT...
THIS MASK IS REALLY...
KEERAKK

...HERE TO HIDE...

...MY *TRUE* FACE!

KRAK

KRAK

!!

Rurouni Kenshin

KLSAAASH

Act 24—Savage Han'nya, Honorable Shikijō

Act 24
Savage Han'nya, Honorable Shikijō

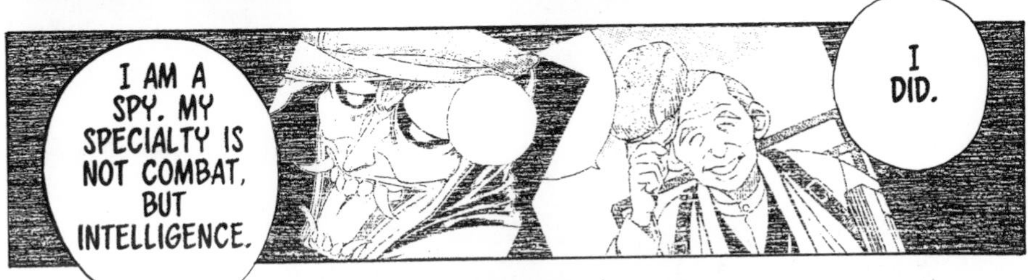

TO BE ABLE TO WEAR *ANY* FACE ATOP MY OWN...

...I BURNED MY LIPS, SLASHED MY EARS...

CUT MY NOSE, CRUSHED MY CHEEKBONES.

BRRR
.....
I DON'T KNOW WHERE *YOU* COME FROM...
...BUT IN *MY* HOME DISTRICT, THERE ARE MANY POOR VILLAGES.

EVEN NOW, THE CUSTOM IS TO KILL ONE'S OWN CHILD, TO LESSEN THE MOUTHS TO FEED.

WHERE I GREW UP WE CALLED IT... "RETURNING THE CHILD."

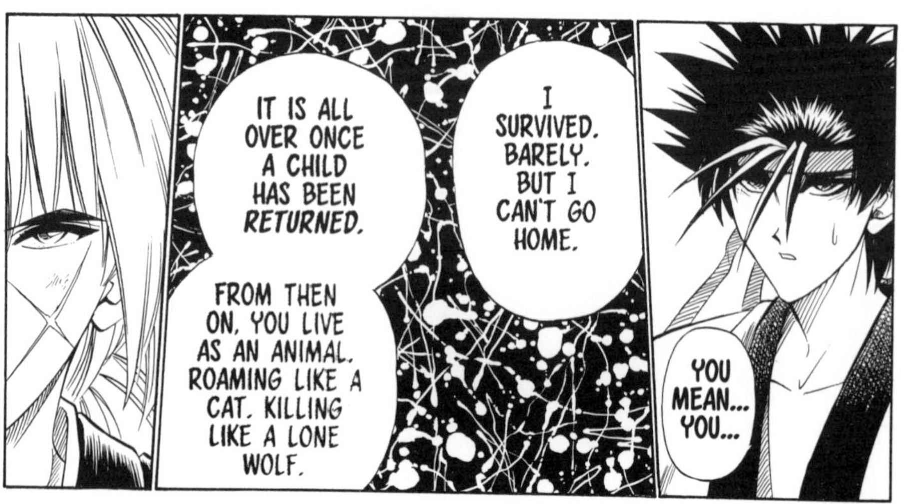

YOU MEAN... YOU...
I SURVIVED. BARELY. BUT I CAN'T GO HOME.
IT IS ALL OVER ONCE A CHILD HAS BEEN *RETURNED.*
FROM THEN ON, YOU LIVE AS AN ANIMAL. ROAMING LIKE A CAT. KILLING LIKE A LONE WOLF.

BUT—!!!
STEEL CLAWS!!
AOSHI FOUND THIS WOLF—AND RESCUED HIM!!
HE TRAINED ME TO BE A FIRST-CLASS ONMITSU!!
HE GAVE ME THE EDO CASTLE ONIWABANSHŪ...
...MY COMRADES... AND MY REASON TO *LIVE*!!

IF I CAN BE OF ANY USE TO AOSHI...
...WHAT NEED HAVE I FOR A FACE?!!!
LOOK OUT, KENSHIN!
THIS IS BAD!!
ALL THIS GUY CARES FOR IS THE ONIWABANSHŪ OKASHIRA!!
HE MAY AS WELL BE A MONSTER!!

THEN ANSWER THIS, HAN'NYA!
THE PAST OF MEGUMI-DONO...
DID YOU KNOW OF IT?!
HSS
HOW CAN YOU ASK THAT?!
THE MASTER SPY OF THE ONIWABANSHŪ ...
...KNOWS ALL!!
GNG

NG?!

RRR

RRR

RRR

RRR

MMUH ...!!

BOM

TCH !

DMM
UWOHHH!
KIEHHH!

SPYOOO...

HMPH.
NOT
GOOD.

BUT STILL YOUR SKILLS...ARE NOTHING... COMPARED TO...

...AOSHI ...

THUD

FINALLY...
HE WAS A TOUGH ONE.
WHEW
...HAN'NYA.

YOU KNOW FULL WELL HOW TERRIBLE SOLITUDE CAN BE.
DID YOU EVER THINK OF WHAT MEGUMI-DONO SUFFERS?

READ THIS WAY

KENSHIN ...
MEGUMI-DONO MAY BE IN NEED.
KEEEN
LET'S HURRY.

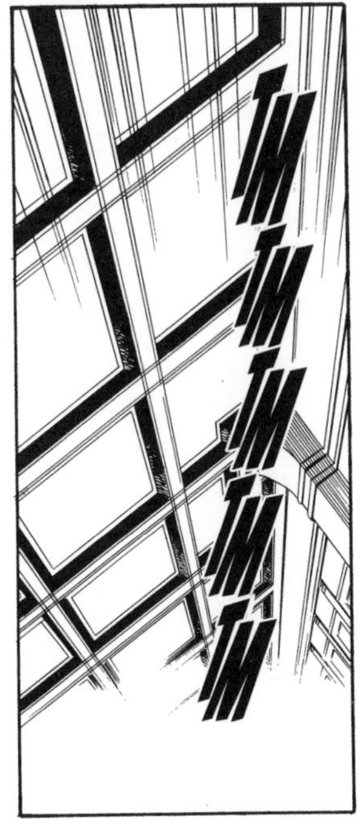

HOW'S THE WOUND?
SHALLOW... AND ALREADY STOPPED BLEEDING.
Yahiko

STILL...
THIS "SHINOMORI AOSHI"...TO GET THAT KIND OF LOYALTY FROM A FIGHTER LIKE HAN'NYA...
WHAT KIND OF A MAN IS HE...?
WHOA.

TNNG
IF YOU'VE COME THIS FAR, YOU'VE DEFEATED HAN'NYA.
YOU MUST BE GOOD.
ZOOOP
!!
悪
TOMM!

KEEPER OF THE CASTLE GATE, EDO...

...SHIKIJŌ.

MY WAY TO SAY HELLO.
HELLO!!

ORAH!
FLIPP
PPPP
!
SANO!
I'M FINE. LEAVE THE MUSCLE-HEAD TO ME.
YOU GUYS KEEP GOING!
THIS GUY I CAN HANDLE EASY. YOU GO GET THAT DRUG-PUSHING WENCH OUT OF HERE!
SANO...
LET'S GO, YAHIKO !!
YEAH!

……
DDDD
ZOP

READ
THIS
WAY

D-D-D-
PFF.

YOU...
YOU PLANNED TO LET KENSHIN GO FROM THE START.

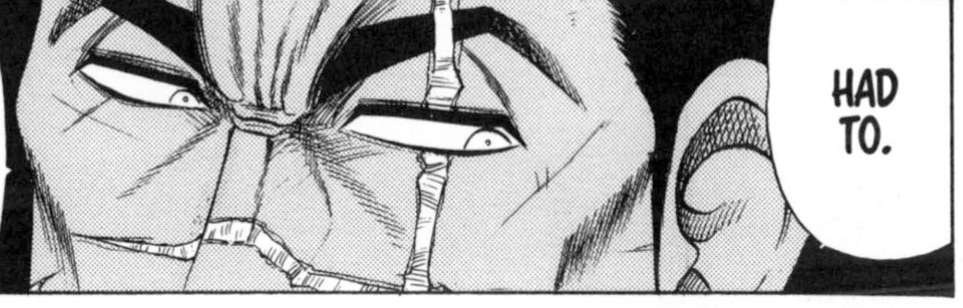
HAD TO.
BEST GUYS GO TO THE BEST GUYS. WAY IT GOES.

ME, I HAVE TO SETTLE FOR THIRD-RATE GOODS...
FOR YOU, "FIGHT MERCHANT ZANZA."

PFFT. NOT SURPRISED, ARE YOU? HAN'NYA DID HIS RESEARCH.
TING
YOU HAD QUITE A REP IN THE TOKYO UNDER-GROUND.

THOUGH WITHOUT THAT BIG OL' ZANBATŌ, YOU AIN'T MUCH.
TNG

DON'T YOU UNDER-ESTIMATE ME...
...YOU GLUED-TOGETHER PIECE O'CRAP!!
THOGG
THE ZANBATŌ'S GONE, YEAH... BUT THE TWO ARMS BEHIND IT ARE STILL HERE!
AND THE ONE SETTLING FOR *THIRD-RATE* HERE...
...IS *ME!!*

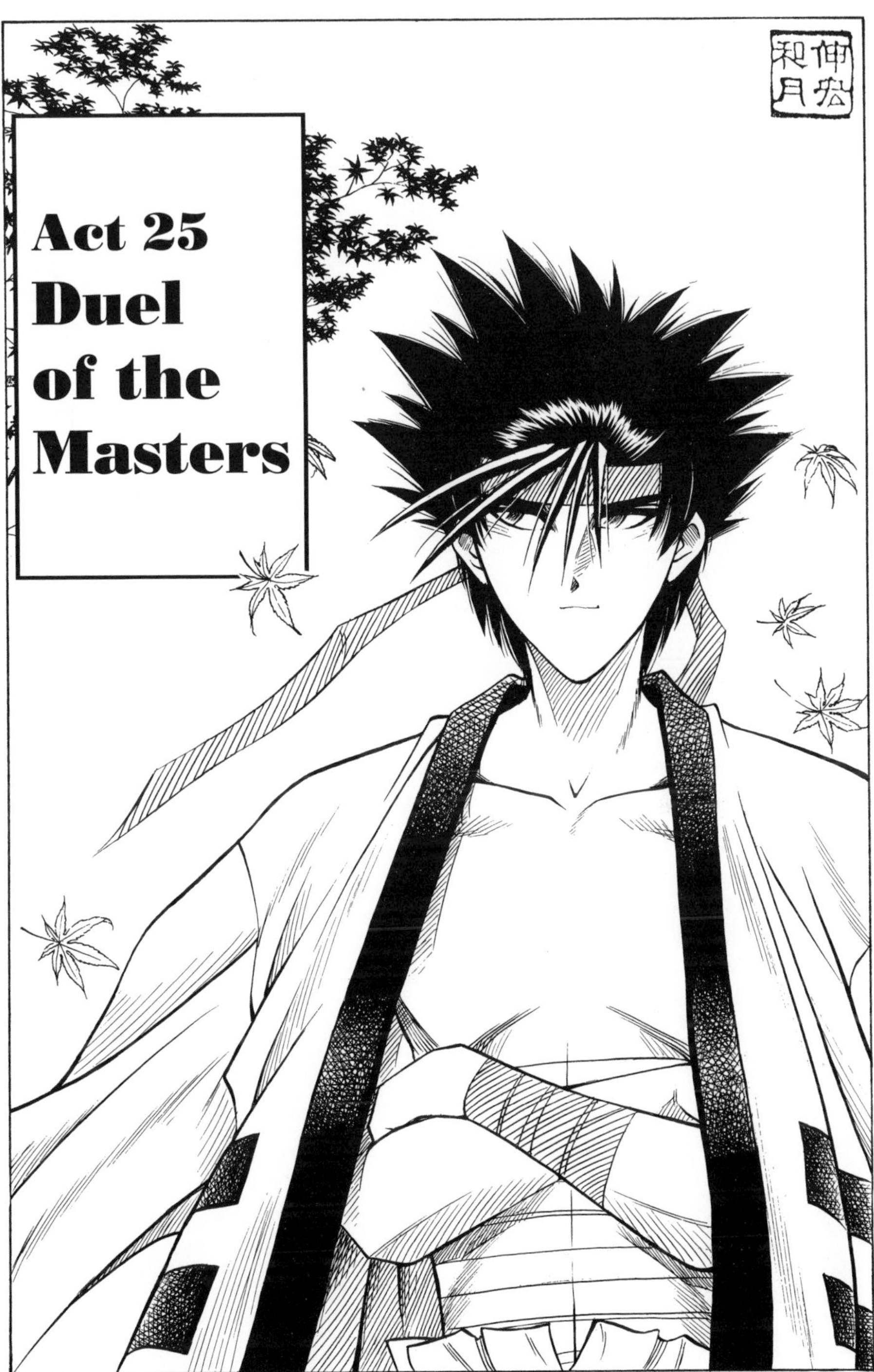

伸弘
和月
Act 25
Duel
of the
Masters

D D D D D D D D

HEY, KENSHIN.
WILL SANOSUKE BE ALL RIGHT ALONE? THAT THUG LOOKED PRETTY TOUGH.
YOU *ARE* TALKING ABOUT SANO. HE'LL BE FINE.
BESIDES, EVEN IF WE WERE THERE, WOULD SANO LET US HELP?
TRUE.
WE'RE GOING IN—GET READY!

Ballroom
BAM
WHAM

PFF. YOU, SETTLE? FOR ME, KEEPER OF THE EDO CASTLE GATE?
LOOKS LIKE WE SHOULD BOTH TAKE OUR TWO PROUD ARMS...
OOOOOOOM
HYAH
KLAKKA
...AND PUT THAT STRENGTH TO THE TEST.

GOOD IDEA. LET'S GO!!
D-D-D-D-DD
ORAH !!!
VVSHHH

GYUROROROO
NNNNG!!!
GH!
THUNKKKKK
THE PIECE O'CRAP HAS MUSCLES ...!!
TCH.

GOOOOOO
UMM

OH. SORRY.
HEH...
DIDN'T MEAN THE HEAD BUTT.

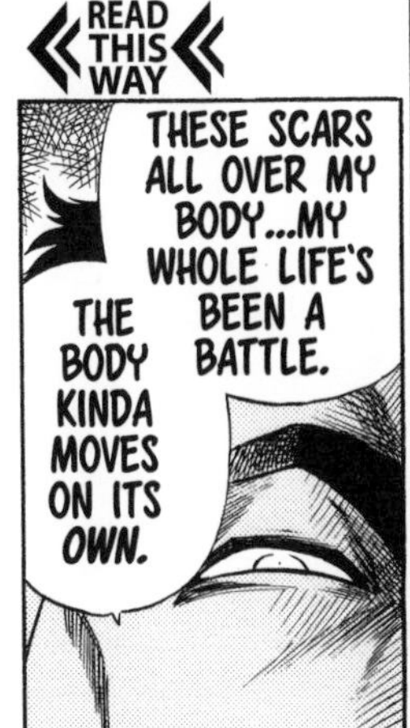

READ THIS WAY
THESE SCARS ALL OVER MY BODY...MY WHOLE LIFE'S BEEN A BATTLE.
THE BODY KINDA MOVES ON ITS *OWN.*

THK

EASY, NOW. IMPRESSIVE YOUR SKULL WASN'T CRUSHED BY THE BLOW...

STILL, YOU TOOK *SOME* DAMAGE.

BETTER COUNT ON BEING WOOZY FOR A WHILE YET.

EVEN SO...

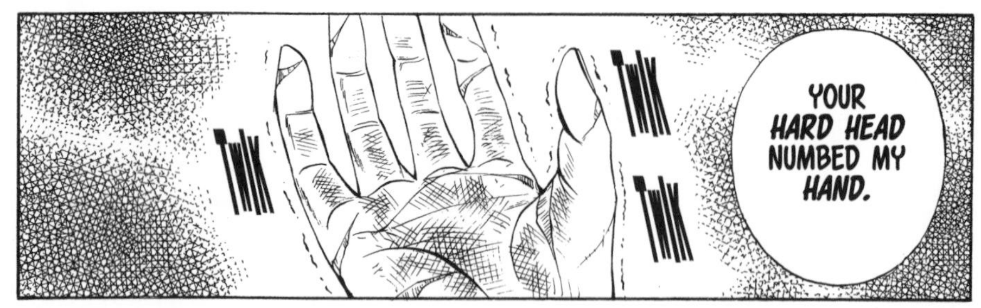
YOUR HARD HEAD NUMBED MY HAND.
TWIK
TWIK
TWIK

THINK I LIKE YOU, KID.
WHY NOT CUT TIES WITH BATTŌSAI...
AND JOIN UP WITH US?

HUH?
ME, I WORKED AS ONMITSU IN SATSUMA.
FOR THE ISHIN SHISHI, OF ALL THINGS.
IF IT'S YOUR PAST, DON'T WORRY.
YOU'RE STRONG. THAT'S ALL THAT COUNTS.

IN THE 2ND YEAR OF KEIŌ, I INFILTRATED EDO CASTLE WITH ORDERS TO GET INFO FOR THE UPCOMING BATTLE.
I WAS DEFEATED BY HE OKASHIRA... HO WAS ONLY 13 AT THE TIME!!

I DO HATE TO WASTE SO MAGNIFICENT A PHYSIQUE.
HUF
HUF
THE MEDICINES OF THE ONIWABANSHŪ CAN MAKE THOSE MUSCLES EVEN *STRONGER.*

JOIN US...AND BECOME UNSTOPPABLE!

Young Aoshi. Although the design was initially for a different character, I tried him out here and he was a big hit (with women, at least...). His bangs, though— man, are they a pain. Man.

AND HE WAS TRUE TO HIS WORD!!
SAME FOR YOU.
NOT THERE YET, BUT YOU *COULD* BE.
USE THE STUFF THEY OFFER, AND BE AS STRONG AS HAN'NYA... EVEN *ME!*
IF WHAT YOU SAY IS TRUE...
...THIS SHINOMORI AOSHI, HE'S QUITE A GUY.
YOU SAID IT! IF IT HAD BEEN *HIM* IN KYOTO HUNTING PATRIOTS...
IT'D BE THE *OKASHIRA* WHO'D BE THE LEGEND, NOT *BATTŌSAI!*
THE ONI-WABANSHŪ IS STRONG, NO DOUBT ABOUT IT.
BESHIMI... HYOTTOKO... DEADLY FIGHTERS, ALL OF YOU.

STILL...

...THAT'S ALL.

.....

SHINOMORI AOSHI SURROUNDS HIMSELF WITH THE STRONGEST OF ALL.

BUT THAT'S *ALL* THEY ARE.

WHAT ...

...DO YOU...?

I *MEAN*, YOU'RE STRONG... BUT NOTHING ELSE.

YOU STAY TOGETHER BECAUSE OF IT. THE *FIGHT* IS EVERYTHING.

BUT HIMURA KENSHIN IS DIFFERENT.

READ THIS WAY

OUR YOUNG MISS...

...YAHIKO...

...TAKANI MEGUMI.

DMM
SO WHAT'RE YOU SAYING, KID?!
KATCH
!!
GRN
GRN
EVERYBODY KNOWS.
KENSHIN *NEVER* WIELDS HIS BLADE FOR *HIMSELF.*
YOU...
KATCH
HIS SAKABATŌ IS THERE TO *PROTECT* PEOPLE.

YOU ONIWABANSHŪ—YOU *DROWN* IN YOUR OWN STRENGTH, *LOWERING* YOURSELVES TO BECOME *PAWNS* OF TAKEDA KANRYŪ!!

COMPARED TO HIMURA KENSHIN, YOU'RE *NOTHING!!*

FOOL...!!

I GIVE YOU ONE COMPLIMENT AND YOU THINK YOU CAN JUDGE *US?!*

DROWNING IN MY OWN STRENGTH, AM I?! *AM I??!*

DM DM DM DM DM DM DM

DEFEAT ME FIRST, *THEN TALK* BIG!!
THIS... IS JUST...

...WHAT I'M TALKING ABOUT, NUMBSKULL !!!
WH-WHAT ?!!

YOUR HEAD'S AS HARD AS MINE, BUT THAT DON'T MEAN EITHER OF 'EM...
...CAN'T BE HURT.
UH... GUH.
ZZZ
UMP
SHIKIJŌ.
YOU EVER GET THE CHANCE, FACE KENSHIN.
TM

READ THIS WAY
MAYBE YOU CAN GET BACK...
...SOMETHING YOU LOST LONG AGO.
HOW MANY MORE ONIWABANSHŪ ARE THERE...?
DM
DM
MORE GUYS LIKE THAT ONE, AND MY BODY WON'T...
DM
...LAST.
DOMP

ZAHH!

READ THIS WAY
WE KNOW EACH OTHER'S FACES. NOW WE SPEAK FOR THE FIRST TIME...
INDEED...

The Secret Life of Characters (10)

—Oniwabanshū • Han'nya—

He's not "Masked Ninja [Akakage]," if that's what you're thinking [*laughs*]. Han'nya's forebears are more like the Elephant Man. Originally, his face was to have been congenitally deformed. Like the Elephant Man, the idea was for him to have been stepped on while still in his mother's body. He would have been treated not as a human being, but as a monster, and would have lived deep in the mountains, in solitude. He'd be discovered by Aoshi, join the Oniwabanshū. He'd be a tragic figure who tells himself, "Only in the Oniwabanshū am I able to live as a human being." Only in battle would he find his raison d'être.

When it came to writing all this up, though, my editor and I got into a discussion about how it might be interpreted to mean "the shape of one's life is determined by how one is born." After a long conversation about whether such a message is even appropriate in a young men's magazine (I think it was the longest discussion since the start of *RuroKen*), I came to the conclusion that a change needed to be made. Han'nya was really a challenging character for me, in that I was aware for perhaps the first time of the responsibility of writing for young people.

Personality-wise, he's based on Yamazaki Susumu of the Shinsengumi. Many readers proposed that, beneath the mask, he was secretly handsome, or was *kagemusha* (a body double) for Aoshi (his twin brother, say!), or even a *kunoichi* (a female ninja). There were lots of interesting guesses. For whatever reason, the idea of a *kunoichi* being part of the Oniwabanshū never entered my head; I find it interesting. Maybe she'll appear as a new character in the future—not that there are any plans as of yet.

The model in terms of design was nothing more than a skeleton. That the left and right eyes are of different shape and size is a remnant of the original concept. As a side note, Han'nya's outfit became more and more blocky as I drew it, leading my assistants to call it "robot," "mobile suit," you name it.

Act 26
Shinomori Aoshi, Okashira

WHAT WAS SAID TO HAN'NYA IS NOW SAID TO YOU...

THIS ONE WOULD *AVOID* BATTLE WHEN POSSIBLE.
WILL YOU NOT LET US PASS AND TELL US WHERE KANRYŪ AND MEGUMI-DONO ARE?
WHEN YOU SAID THAT TO HAN'NYA, DID HE LET YOU PASS?
HE *DIDN'T*, DID HE?

ASK FOR THEIR LOCATION WITH YOUR SAKABATŌ.
MY REPLY SHALL COME WITH THIS.
THE LENGTH OF THE BLADE...!

YOU THINK YOU CAN FIGHT US WITH A SINGLE WAKIZASHI?!
HOW ARROGANT ARE YOU?!!
HAVE THE CHILD STAND BACK.
HEY!!
THIS ONE ASKS IT AS WELL.
......
IT'S JUST... Y'KNOW.

FOOEY TO BOTH OF YOU!
FOOEY!
JUST DON'T WASTE TIME WITH A WAKIZASHI, YOU HEAR?!
HURRY AND FINISH IT!
PING

ZAH
NO...IF IN FACT THAT ACTUALLY IS A WAKIZASHI.
IT IS A KODACHI...
SSIP
DO YOU KNOW ITS PROPERTIES?
KODACHI?
A MIDSIZED SWORD, BETWEEN A KATANA AND WAKIZASHI.

THE "SHIELD-SWORD"—THAT'S HOW THE KODACHI* IS KNOWN.

ITS LENGTH PROVIDES LESS POWER, BUT ITS LIGHTNESS AND EASE OF USE MAKE FOR A FINE DEFENSE.

TO BE ON ITS OTHER END...

IS QUITE A CHALLENGE.

......

*ALSO, Ō- (LONG) WAKIZASHI, OR NAGA- (LONG) WAKIZASHI

MEANING... I TAKE THE OFFENSIVE.

YES.

WH...?

!!
FAST!
GANG

KENSHIN!
A KICK?!
IS THIS MAN...
...LIKE HAN'NYA...
...ALSO A MARTIAL ARTIST?!!

DADADADADADADADA
GG...
SHOOO
SHOOO
SHOOO
KEEN
KEEN
KEEN
TM

READ THIS WAY

!
DM
AH. YOU USE THE KODACHI TO CREATE AN IMPENETRA-BLE GUARD...
THEN ATTACK WITH MARTIAL ARTS, LIKE HAN'NYA.

YOU MAKE ONE MISTAKE.
I FIGHT NOT LIKE HAN'NYA, BUT *HE* LIKE *ME*.

HIS BLOWS CANNOT COMPARE TO HIS *MASTER'S*.
A *MISTAKE* TO THINK THEM THE SAME.
TM
WOBBLE
KKH...

IT'S NOTHING PERSONAL, BATTŌSAI.

WHEN YOU DIE, IT WILL BE AS *FIRST* AMONG ALL THE ISHIN SHISHI.

...

YOU DON'T FIGHT FOR KANRYŪ, THEN, ANY OF YOU.

OF COURSE NOT. WHO CARES WHAT HAPPENS TO THAT SCUM?

AS ONIWABANSHŪ OF EDO CASTLE, THEN.

FOR THE TOKUGAWA BAKUFU, CRUSHED BY THE REVOLUTION.

THEN, BEING A PATRIOT, YOU MUST KNOW OF THE ACTS OF TOKUGAWA YOSHINOBU, AT THE *BATTLE OF TOBA FUSHIMI.*

YES...
THE LAST TOKUGAWA SHŌGUN, YOSHINOBU, KNOWING HIS FORCES WERE OUTNUMBERED, *FLED* OSAKA CASTLE WITH HIS SENIOR OFFICERS ON HIS WARSHIP, TO EDO...
LEAVING BEHIND 10,000 MEN TO FIGHT AND DIE ON THE BATTLEFIELD.

ONCE AT EDO, HE SOUGHT SANCTUARY AT THE KAN-EIJI TEMPLE IN UENO, ENTRUSTING ALL TO KATSU KAISHŪ...
WHO, IN CONFERENCE WITH SAIGŌ TAKAMORI, AGREED TO AVOID BATTLE AT EDO CASTLE.
EDO, THE KEY CASTLE OF ALL, WAS TAKEN WITHOUT BLOODSHED.

THUS ENDED THE BAKUMATSU, WITHOUT THE ONIWABANSHŪ *EVER* SEEING COMBAT.

WE CARE NOTHING FOR THE COWARD TOKUGAWA. OUR REGRET IS ONLY THAT WE COULD NOT FIGHT.

THE FLOW OF TIME OFFERS NO "WHAT IFS."

AND YET, IF THERE *HAD* BEEN A BATTLE...

...IF WE *HAD* FOUGHT AT EDO...THE ISHIN SHISHI VICTORY WOULD HAVE BEEN *OURS.*

WE'D HAVE SET A GREAT FIRE THERE, WE ONIWABANSHŪ, STRIKING IN THE CONFUSION AT THE HEART OF THE OPPOSITION FORCES—AT THE PATRIOTS SAIGŌ, ŌKUBO, AND KATSURA—PUTTING THEM TO DEATH.
THE REMAINDER WOULD HAVE BEEN A HEADLESS MOB, EASILY CRUSHED BY OUR OWN ARMY.

N-NO WAY! THAT'D BE *IMPOSSIBLE* !!
OH NO IT'S NOT. EVEN NOW, IT'S NOT.
EVEN *HERE*, IN TOKYO...
HE'S...

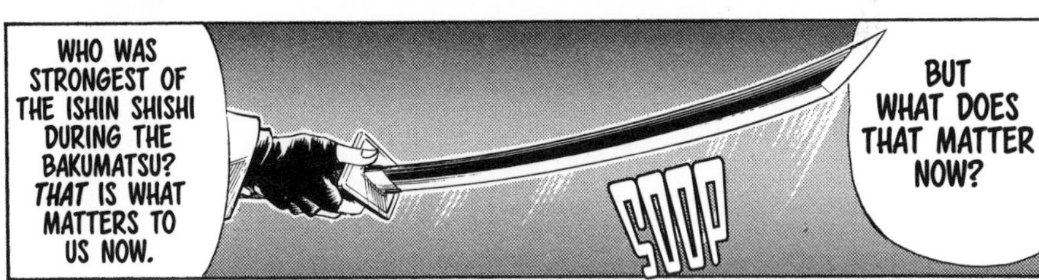

BUT WHAT DOES THAT MATTER NOW?
SOOP
WHO WAS STRONGEST OF THE ISHIN SHISHI DURING THE BAKUMATSU? *THAT* IS WHAT MATTERS TO US NOW.

WE ONIWABANSHŪ.

THAT, I SHALL PROVE.

BACK THEN...

ISHIN SHISHI, SAMURAI OF THE BAKUFU, ALL THROWN INTO BATTLE.
WE FOUGHT...BUT IT WASN'T TO PROVE WHO WAS IN THE RIGHT, WHO WAS IN THE WRONG.
WE LAID DOWN OUR LIVES FOR THE COUNTRY'S FUTURE, FOR THE PEACE AND HAPPINESS OF THE PEOPLE.
BUT NOT YOU!! YOU, WHO SPEAK SO CASUALLY OF BURNING THE CITY!
THERE'S NOTHING LEFT IN YOU BUT THE ICE-COLD BLOOD OF WAR.
EVEN NOW, BECAUSE OF IT...
YOU CONTINUE TO CAUSE SUFFERING, TO MEGUMI-DONO AND TO THE PEOPLE POISONED BY OPIUM!
SOOP
!

AS ISHIN SHISHI—OR EVEN AS RUROUNI—
—THIS ONE WILL NOT STAND IDLY BY!!
ZANNG
SAY WHAT YOU WILL.
SINCERE OR NOT, YOU'VE NO CHANCE TO WIN.
COME.
PFT

ABOVE !!
KNG

THE *RYŪTSUISEN* OF THE HITEN MITSURUGI SCHOOL, FOLLOWED BY *BATTŌJUTSU*— WITHOUT WAITING TO LAND.

QUITE AN ATTACK.

BUT MY KODACHI IS NOT SO *FLIMSY* AS TO BE DEFEATED BY THAT.

DAMN HIM!!
BAM
THAT MAN, A MERE HIRELING, HAS INSULTED ME!!
HF
HF
HF

AT LEAST...NOW I KNOW! HE'S JUST LIKE BATTŌSAI— HE CAN'T BE BOUGHT WITH MONEY. AND HE LOVES FIGHTING, TO THE POINT OF INSANITY.
HF
HF
HF
IF ANYTHING GOES WRONG— HE COULD TURN ON ME!!

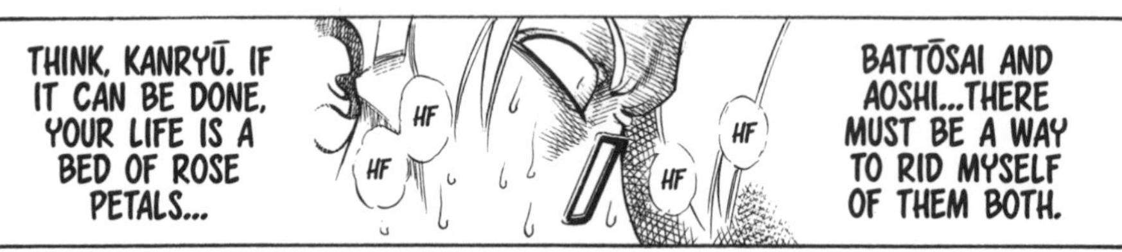
BATTŌSAI AND AOSHI...THERE MUST BE A WAY TO RID MYSELF OF THEM BOTH.
HF
HF
HF
HF
THINK, KANRYŪ. IF IT CAN BE DONE, YOUR LIFE IS A BED OF ROSE PETALS...

UMM... KANRYŪ-SAN?
KREE
WHAT?! WHAT DO YOU WANT?!
WELL...UH... THE "DEVICE" IS SCHEDULED FOR A TEST-RUN TONIGHT. WHAT SHOULD WE—
IDIOT! REVIEW THE SITUATION AND MAKE YOUR OWN DECISION. WHAT'S A CAPTAIN FOR?!

READ THIS WAY
O-OF COURSE, SIR. IF YOU'LL EXCUSE ME...
HF
HF
WAIT RIGHT THERE!!
AARGH...
—
GASP
THAT'S IT!!
AHHA!
I'VE GOT THAT, DON'T I?!
HWOOOOO
I'M RUNNING THIS TEST— WHERE IS IT?!
THE...THE BASEMENT... THE HIDDEN ROOM...
A LIFE OF SUFFERING...
.....
...OR A PEACEFUL DEATH.

The Secret Life of Characters (11)

—Oniwabanshū • Shikijō—

Shikijō's model is Sanosuke. Shocking to hear, perhaps, but true. His personality, then, is similar (cocksure and proud, but also generous), as is his fighting style (powerful), as well as his philosophy (supportive of his "number one"). By putting them on opposite sides and having them fight, I wanted Shikijō and Sanosuke to clearly embody the differences between the two sides. That was the idea behind the fight (which may or may not have worked, but...).

Han'nya wasn't a character you could describe as "evil," but even though Shikijō *was* set up as the complete villain, it was perhaps the noble manner of his conduct that transformed him into a pretty cool guy. He does have an enthusiastic group of fans...but, then again, so do all the Oniwabanshū. For this volume, though, the best response was for the young Aoshi. I guess what matters most in a man is his face [*laughs*].

For his design, there was no specific model. Since he's a "power fighter," I made him all muscles—but that didn't really make him strange-enough looking—so I also gave him scars all over, along with superhero-like, exaggerated musculature.

Act 27—Battle's Heat

Act 27
Battle's Heat

HE'S GOOD...

EVEN *KENSHIN* AS HE IS CAN'T LAND A BLOW ON HIM.

ALSO...

GET UP.

I'D RATHER NOT FINISH SOMEONE WHEN THEY'RE DOWN.

...EVEN WHEN HE'S *WINNING*, HE SHOWS NO EMOTION. THE "ICE-COLD BLOOD OF WAR"...

RRG... MY LEGS ARE FROZEN...
KENSHIN!!
NO NEED FOR WORRY.
WOBBLE
TO LOSE NOW... WHAT WOULD MEGUMI-DONO THINK?
HOW COULD I EVER FACE KAORU-DONO?
NEVER MIND WHAT SANO WOULD SAY.
BESIDES...
...THE COUNTER TO THAT KODACHI IS FINALLY BECOMING CLEAR.
A BLUFF...
TM
YOU SHOULD BE CAREFUL WHAT YOU BRAG ABOUT.

TM
NOT UNLESS YOU CAN SHOW ME...
...HOW YOU PLAN TO DO IT.
TM
TM
TM
TM
TM
HYAH.
TOO SLOW!

KEE
EE
EEEN

WHAT—?!

THE BASE OF THE BLADE...!

UGH ...!!
ZFZF
KNH.
AOSHI.
THE SECRET OF YOUR STRENGTH LIES IN HOW COMPLETELY YOU CONTROL YOUR OPPONENT'S RANGE.
RANGE...
OKAY, YAHIKO. ABOUT RANGE...
IT'S THE DISTANCE IN WHICH YOU CAN ATTACK IN *ONE MOVEMENT*.
SO?!
THE RANGE VARIES WITH EACH INDIVIDUAL'S WEAPON AND SKILL.
YOU WANNA LEARN OR NOT?
IF SO, SHUT UP.
BETWEEN THE MOST SKILLED OF FIGHTERS, VICTORY USUALLY COMES DOWN TO HOW WELL YOU KEEP YOUR OPPONENT *OUT* OF *YOUR* ZONE, AND *STAY* WITHIN YOUR *OWN*.

AT FIRST GLANCE, IT WOULD SEEM THE ONE WITH THE KATANA HOLDS THE ADVANTAGE.

BUT LONGER RANGES ALSO HAVE MORE *BLIND SPOTS.*

YOU USE KODACHI AGAINST KATANA WITHIN THIS ONE'S BLIND SPOT, THEN ATTACK WITH YOUR FIST.

BUT IF THE RANGE OF THE KATANA IS ALTERED TO THAT OF THE *KODACHI...*

...THE BLIND SPOT NATURALLY...

...SHRINKS.

.....

I SEE. THE KATANA SHOWS ITS SHARPNESS BY PUSHING OR PULLING AGAINST THE TARGET.

IF YOU SIMPLY GRASP IT, ESPECIALLY AT THE BASE WHERE IT'S MOST DULL, IT WON'T DIG INTO THE BONE.

BLUP

BLUP

BREAK THE BONE BY LETTING THE FLESH BE CUT... IS IT?

SWAAY...

I HAVE SEEN THE *TRUE ESSENCE* OF THE HITOKIRI.

AS A GIFT IN RETURN...

...I WILL ALLOW YOU TO SEE THE ESSENCE OF THE ONIWABANSHŪ OKASHIRA.

!

WAFT

HYOO

SO SLOW—?!

GACCH

WHY NOT FASTER?

!!

SWAYYY

!!
SWAY
THIS IS...
SWORD-DANCE?!
VWOO
KNK
NOT RITUAL DANCE...
SWAY
...BUT COMBAT DANCE, COMBINING YOUR KODACHI SKILL AND MARTIAL ARTS MOVEMENT!
SHINOMORI AOSHI'S TRUE FIGHTING STYLE...!!
SWAY
DON'T BOTHER. YOU, SO USED TO SWORDFIGHTING IN WHICH STILLNESS AND MOVEMENT ARE CLEAR AS NIGHT AND DAY..
SWAY
...YOU WILL NEVER "GET" MY FLOWING MOVEMENT.
VWOO

READ THIS WAY
SWAY
DIE.

KENSHIN !!
KAITEN KENBU*...
USED TO FINISH ALL WHO WOULD INTRUDE UPON EDO CASTLE.
*KAITEN KENBU="DANCE OF THE WHEELING SWORD"

IT'S OVER, LAD.
HIMURA BATTŌSAI IS DEAD.
GNG
SHUT UP!! YOU GET ME NEXT!
EVEN IF IT MEANS I DIE...
...AT LEAST YOU'LL GO WITH ME!!
HYAH

...STRONG SPIRIT.
I'M ALMOST SORRY TO KILL YOU.

YAHIKO IS...AN IMPORTANT PART OF KAMIYA KASSHIN-RYŪ...

GNG GNG GNG...

NO WAY HE... DIES HERE.

!

KENSHIN!

GNG...

OR *THIS ONE* EITHER, FOR THAT MATTER.

AFRAID NOT.

HF

KREE

KREE

KREE

HF

HF

WOBBLE

HF

HF

HF

HF

HF

ARE YOU IMMORTAL, OR...?!

READ THIS WAY

KEE-RAKK

YOUR KAITEN KENBU...

...CUT THROUGH THE METAL SHEATH LIKE WOOD.

HF

HF

HF

I SEE...SO YOU PULLED IN THE SCABBARD, TAKING ONLY HALF-DAMAGE.

QUITE A MAN. THERE'S A REASON YOU'RE CALLED MOST POWERFUL.

I ACKNOWLEDGE IT...FROM THE DEPTHS OF MY HEART.

BUT NOW...

NOW IS WHEN I MAKE THAT TITLE OURS!!

JAB!

SWAAAY

AY-AY-AY...
HF
HF
HF

KENSHIN, BE CAREFUL!
THE SWORD-DANCE IS COMING AGAIN!!
I'VE TOLD YOU—THIS FLOWING MOVEMENT IS BEYOND YOU.
ESPECIALLY NOW THAT YOU ARE BADLY WOUNDED AND SLOWED.
HUF
HUF

READ THIS WAY
IT'S OVER, HIMURA BATTŌSAI!!
HAAH
KANG
KENSHIN!!!

YOUR MOVEMENT MAY BE "BEYOND," IT'S TRUE...

HF

HF

HF

...BUT THE MOMENT YOU *ATTACK* FROM YOUR SWORD-DANCE, IT'S A DIFFERENT STORY.

DAPPPP!

THE *BLADE-CATCH!!*
THE ONE AND ONLY BARE-HANDED MOVE COMMON TO *ALL* 500 KENJUTSU SWORD STYLES.
WHILE MARTIAL ARTS, ON THE OTHER HAND, HAS NOT A *ONE.*
BLUP
BLUP

AOSHI, IF YOU WANT THE TITLE "MOST POWERFUL" SO MUCH, *HAVE* IT.
HUF
HUF
HUF
IT'S JUST ONE MORE BURDEN TO CARRY.

FOR THIS ONE...
THE ONLY THINGS THAT MATTER...
GB
...ARE THOSE WHO ARE WAITING, AND THOSE WHO NEED...

...THIS ONE'S *HELP!*

!!

Act 28
Battle's End

DOM
H... HUK...
CAN I... LOSE?
DON'T FORCE YOURSELF! GET BACK!
EVEN YOU CAN'T TAKE TWO BLOWS TO THE THROAT.
HF
HF

IT'S NOT OVER!!
KENSHIN!!

DMM

KENSHIN!

TM TM

ZDZZZ

IS HE DEAD...?
NO... BUT HE'S OUT.

HIS THROAT BADLY DAMAGED FROM TWO HARD HITS...
STILL HE WANTED TO HIT BACK... SO HE TRIED A DEEP BREATH.
MEANING EXTREME PAIN AND ASPHYXIATION.

IN THE END...
THOUGH HIS HEART NEVER ACCEPTED DEFEAT...
...DEFEAT ACCEPTED HIM.
.....
PAT

WHEN HIS KAITEN KENBU HIT FULL FORCE...
...WHAT YOU SAID THEN...
IT WAS VERY COMFORTING.
HEH
HEH HEH HEH!
ALL RIGHT! NOW ALL THAT'S LEFT TO DO IS BEAT UP KANRYŪ AND RESCUE MEGUMI!
BRING IT ON!
A FINE THOUGHT... IF WE KNEW WHERE SHE WAS.
PERHAPS IF AOSHI WERE AWAKE...
SWAY
!

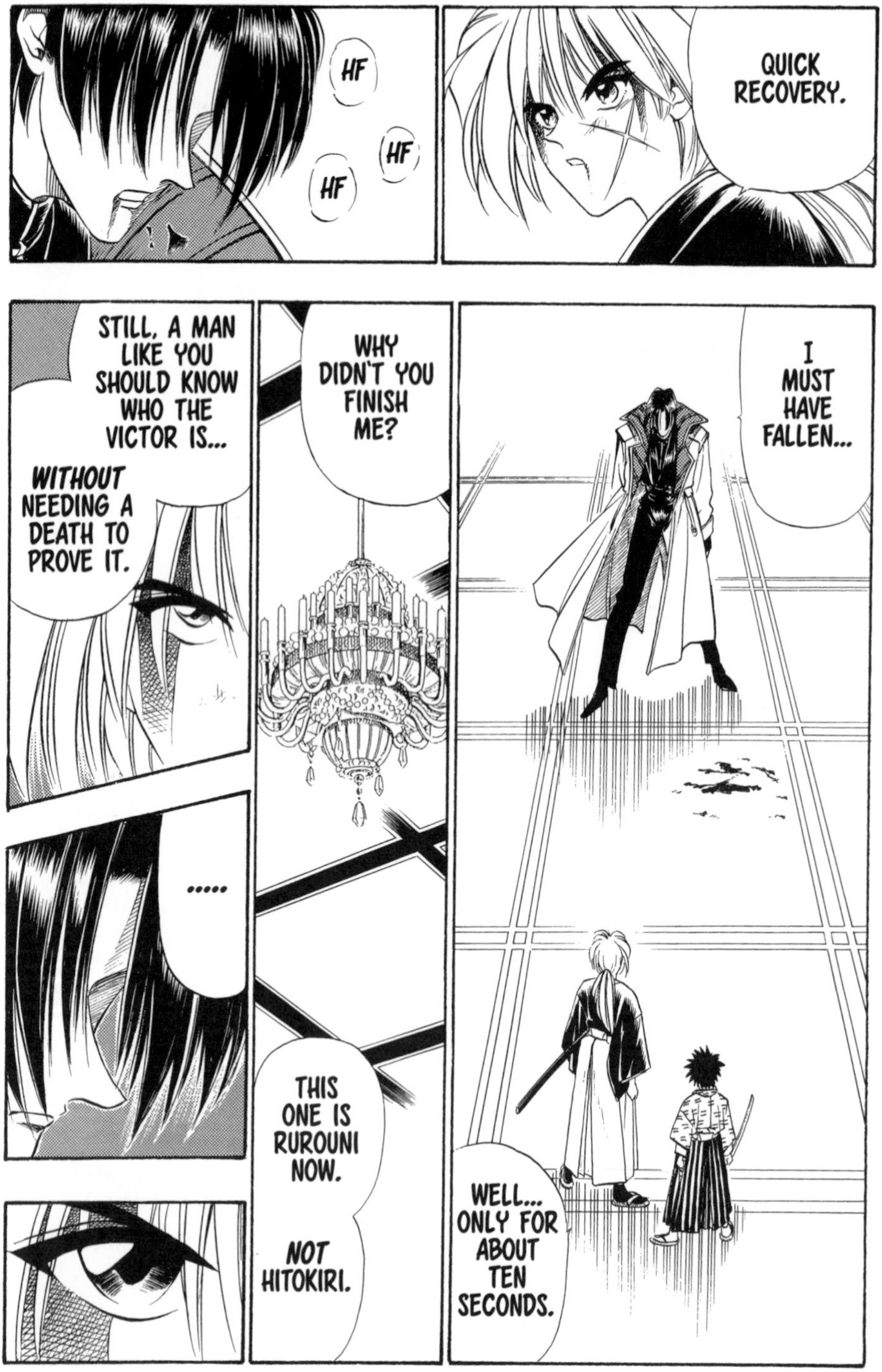

QUICK RECOVERY.

HF
HF
HF

I MUST HAVE FALLEN...

WELL... ONLY FOR ABOUT TEN SECONDS.

WHY DIDN'T YOU FINISH ME?

STILL, A MAN LIKE YOU SHOULD KNOW WHO THE VICTOR IS...

WITHOUT NEEDING A DEATH TO PROVE IT.

.....

THIS ONE IS RUROUNI NOW.

NOT HITOKIRI.

AOSHI, ANSWER ONE QUESTION.

THOUGH YOU'VE ALWAYS BEEN OF THE SHADOWS, YOU'VE ALSO BEEN *OKASHIRA* OF THE ONIWABANSHŪ.

SURELY YOU MUST HAVE HAD CHANCES TO BECOME A MILITARY OFFICER.

IF YOU NEEDED A PLACE TO PUT YOUR STRENGTHS TO USE, THERE MUST HAVE BEEN OTHER PLACES TO DO SO.

WHY ARE YOU ACTING LIKE SOME HIRED BODYGUARD?

OF COURSE, PLENTY OF THEM. I DON'T KNOW HOW OR WHERE THEY HEARD OF THE ONIWABANSHŪ, BUT EVERYTHING FROM ARMY INTELLIGENCE TO LEADER PROTECTION'S BEEN OFFERED.

EVERY OFFER, THOUGH, WAS FOR ME ALONE.

MEN STRONG IN A SINGLE SKILL—LIKE BESHIMI OR HYOTTOKO—OR MEN LIKE SHIKIJŌ, WHO IS A TRAITOR...

NOT TO MENTION HAN'NYA, WITH HIS TERRIBLE FACE...

FOR THE REST OF THE ONIWABANSHŪ, NO INVITATIONS WERE OFFERED.

HOW COULD I, THE *OKASHIRA*, ABANDON MY OWN MEN?
HOW COULD I?

SHOULD I BE LIKE YOSHINOBU, THE LAST TOKUGAWA SHŌGUN, WHO ENDED AN AGE?
NO. I WILL NOT.
TOKUGAWA YOSHINOBU...
I UNDERSTAND IT, HIS COMPLETE SURRENDER.
IN THE END, IT WAS A POLITICAL DECISION, MEANT TO SAVE THE COUNTRY FROM FURTHER DESTRUCTIVE CONFLICT.
EVEN SO...
...STILL I WILL NOT.
......

IT'S BEEN TEN YEARS SINCE WE ONI-WABANSHŪ WERE THRUST INTO THIS NEW AGE, MEIJI, AND THIS NEW CAPITAL, TOKYO...

ONE BY ONE, I WATCHED THEM FIND NEW WAYS OF LIVING.

UNTIL ONLY FOUR WERE LEFT.

SUCH WERE THE ONIWABANSHŪ OF EDO CASTLE.

THEY LIVED TO FIGHT, YET WERE BARRED FROM IT.

I WANTED THE TITLE, "MOST POWERFUL," FOR THEM...

TO LAY IT BY THEIR SIDE. TO GIVE THEM PRIDE.

FINISH ME.

OR ELSE, IN THE FUTURE, I WILL KEEP COMING AFTER YOU.

THEN COME, IF YOU WILL. UNTIL YOU'RE SATISFIED.
KENSHIN!
BUT BATTLES INVOLVING INNOCENTS WILL *NOT* BE TOLERATED.

.....

HAH, HA HA! SHINOMORI AOSHI, ROLLING OVER TO BEG, AFTER BARKING SO VERY LOUD!!

BAM

!

READ THIS WAY

HIYA.

YOU FOOLS WERE TAKING SO LONG WITH YOUR CHIT-CHAT...

I COULDN'T WAIT. I CAME ON OUT.

HEH

KANRYŪ.....

GOOD. NOW THERE'S NO NEED TO FIND YOU.

SO VERY COCKY!

BUT!

HOW COCKY WILL YOU BE... AFTER SEEING *THIS*?!!

FWAH

WHAT THE HECK ...?!

!

THAT'S ...

FAFF

IT CAN'T BE...

Gatling Gun

Together with the armored ship *Stonewall Jackson* and the Armstrong gun, it is one of the three great machines of war. Invented by an American doctor named Gatling in 1861, the Gatling gun served as the original model for the machine gun. After the Union Army saw astonishing success with this gun during the American Civil War, various models were built and ultimately spread throughout the world. In Japan, the Echigo Nagaoka domain obtained it, and in the third (Northern) battle of the Boshin War, Minister Kawai Tsugunosuke operated it himself, posing a significant threat to the Imperial Army.

READ THIS WAY

OH, VERY GOOD! YOU KNOW YOUR WEAPONS!
SWOOP
BUT DO YOU KNOW THAT THIS IS A *NEW* MODEL, SOLD ON THE BLACK MARKET, WHICH EVEN THE *GOVERNMENT* HASN'T SEEN?!
THE OLD GUNS OF THE BAKUMATSU DON'T EVEN COME *CLOSE*.
SHALL WE GIVE IT A TRY?
GAAATATATATATATATATATAT

OH!
ARE THOSE ...
GUN-SHOTS?
WH-WHAT?
IT'S NOT...
...KEN-SAN...?
...SO LOUD... WHAT WAS THAT?
UGHH
TWIK
WELL, IT WOKE ME UP, ANYWAY...

READ THIS WAY

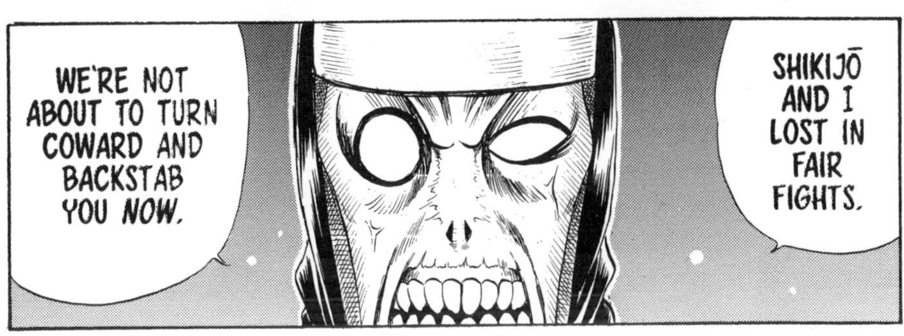

BESIDES, I'M WORRIED FOR AOSHI. I'M GOING WITH SHIKIJŌ, WHAT ABOUT YOU?
TM
TM
YOU'RE...
...NOT *ALL* EVIL, ARE YOU?
HMPH.
WAS THAT SARCASM JUST NOW?
NOT AT ALL.
WAKE UP, SHIKIJŌ.
MMM...

HEY, SHORTY.

WHAT, FATSO?

WHAT DO YOU THINK?! ISN'T IT GREAT?!!
200 SHOTS A MINUTE!! THINK ABOUT IT!!
......
THAT JERK! HE'S MISSING ON PURPOSE, JUST TO WATCH US SQUIRM! CAN'T YOU DO ANYTHING?!
THERE MAY BE ONE CHANCE...
BUT FOR NOW, WE CAN'T DO MUCH BUT RUN.
RUN FAST!
IF YOU STOP, I'LL HIT YOU!!
KANRYŪ!
HOW DID YOU GET SUCH A WEAPON?!

THAT'S KANRYŪ SIR, YOU IMPUDENT FOOL!
!!
AOSHI!
TH
OF ALL THE...
I'LL THINK ABOUT ANSWERING... AFTER A BREAK.
STRIK

I'VE NO INTENTION OF ENDING MY LIFE AS SOME PETTY, SMALL-TIME OPIUM DEALER.

MY GOAL'S *ALWAYS* BEEN TO MOVE ON UP TO THE *BIG TIME.*

YOU MEAN ...

NNG NNG...

A "MERCHANT OF DEATH." AN ARMS DEALER.

AMASSING CAPITAL WITH THE NEW OPIUM...
LEADING WITH THIS NEW-MODEL GATLING GUN, ENTERING THE FIELD WITH A *BANG!*
THUS IS THE STORY OF THE GREAT MERCHANT TAKEDA KANRYŪ TOLD!

AND YOU'RE WILLING...
...TO USE PEOPLE'S LIVES AND HAPPINESS FOR YOUR OWN FORTUNE?
I DON'T EXPECT THE LIKES OF YOU TO UNDERSTAND.
PFFF
HIMURA BATTŌSAI, HOW MANY YEARS DID IT TAKE FOR YOU TO ACHIEVE THOSE SUPERIOR SKILLS?
IT MUST NOT HAVE BEEN AN EASY TASK.

BUT WITH MONEY...I CAN EASILY BUY POWER TO DWARF YOURS!!
ALL AT ONCE!
WITHOUT HAVING TO GIVE UP ANYTHING!
MONEY!!
THAT IS THE SOURCE OF TRUE POWER!
CHCHAKKK
IN THE END, THE "MOST POWERFUL"... IS ME!
DIE!!

DDDP
?!!
WHAT IS THAT?!!
DM
SKID SKID SKID SKID SKID SKID SKID SK
!
A GATLING GUN!!
!!
DAMN!!
SHIKIJŌ!

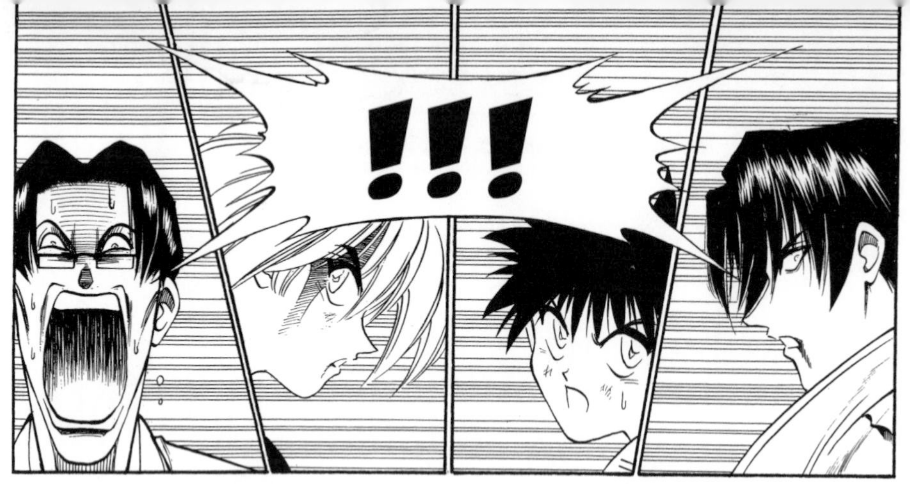
!!!

NOW!

RUN, BATTŌSAI!

!

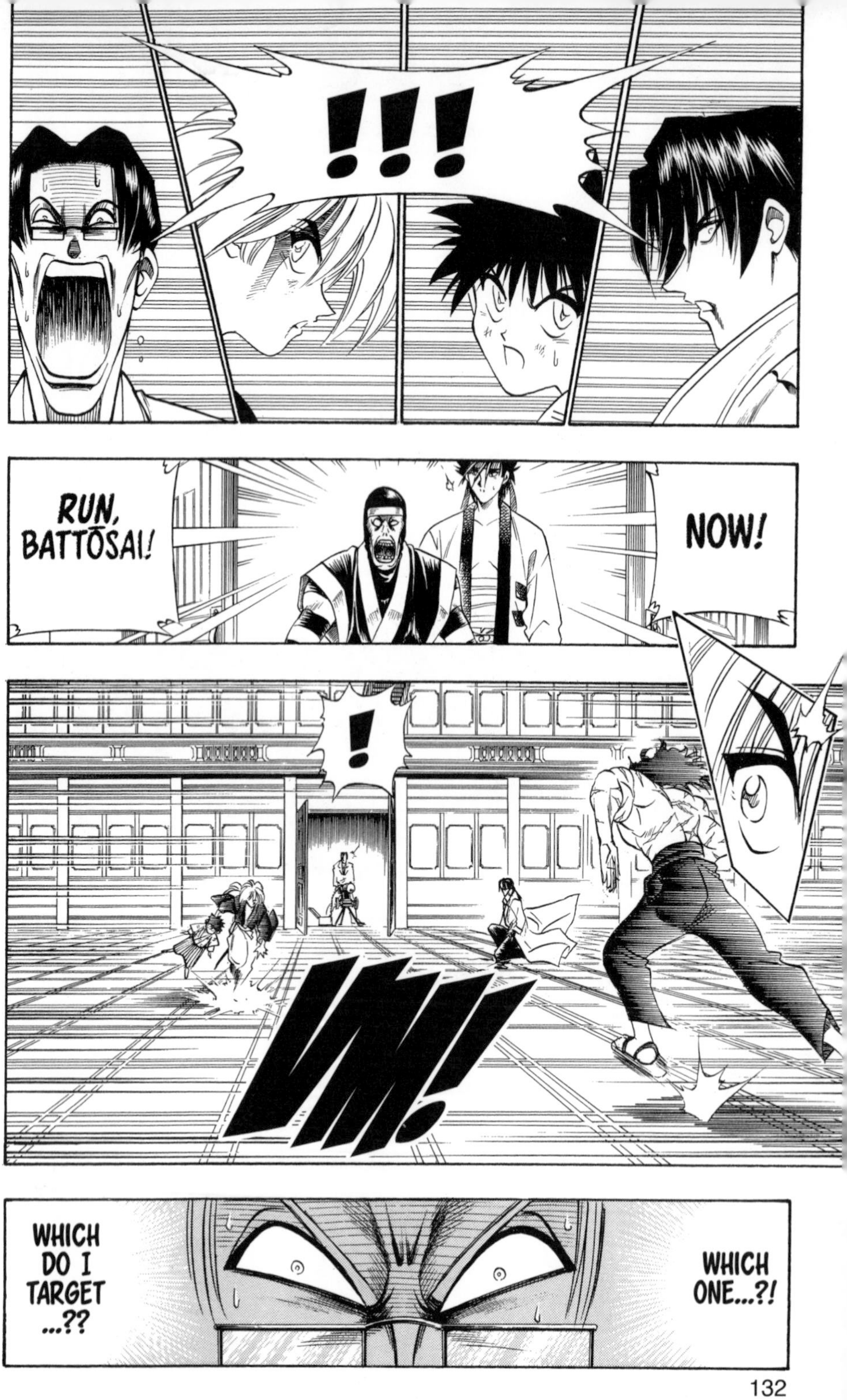

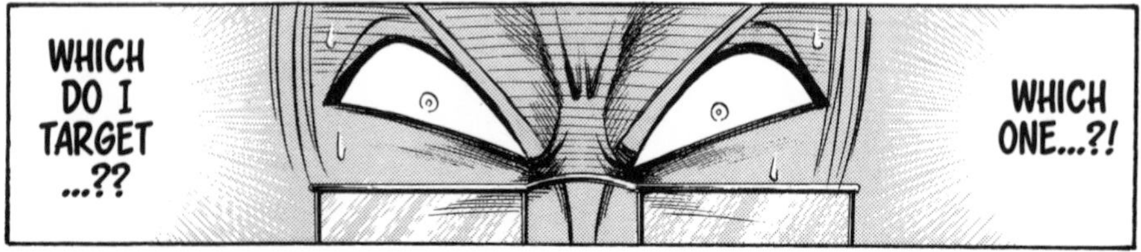
WHICH ONE...?!
WHICH DO I TARGET ...??

READ THIS WAY

THAT BIRDHEAD...
...HE THINKS PRETTY HIGHLY OF YOU.

I DON'T LIKE HIM, BUT HE'S ALL RIGHT.
TAKE GOOD CARE OF HIM.
YOU...

I'LL START WITH THE ONE WHO CAN'T MOVE...AOSHI!
OH NO, YOU DON'T!

SHIKIJŌ !!
SHIKI...
WHOA, HEY...DON'T YOU START SQUIRTING NOW.
DMM
I GOT NO COMPLAINTS. LOOK AT THESE MUSCLES...WHAT MORE COULD I WANT?
NOT EVEN BULLETS CAN...GET THROUGH TO... SHOWED HIM...

SHIKIJŌ...
AT 200 SHOTS A MINUTE...
I CAN CHOP THAT MEATBALL INTO HASH!
HOLD YOUR FIRE!
BAM
!
YOUR OPPONENT NOW...
...IS ME, HYOTTOKO!!
WHAT?!
VWIN
BETTER NOT SHOOT...
...NOT UNLESS YOU WANT THIS OIL BAG TO GO UP IN A FIREBALL!
SPOIN

THEN WHAT IF I SHOOT HERE?!

!

PWMP

HYOTTOKO !!

HEH HEH.

YOU FELL FOR IT.

BESHIMI !!

DOOM

TAKE THIS! POISON RASEN—

HUH?!!

—BYO...

TATATATA

UWAH !!

GATA

TATATATATATA

THUD

BESHIMI!

O-OKASHIRA, WE...WE COULDN'T DO IT...

BLUP

BLUP

BLUP

THEY CALLED US USELESS, SAID WE HAD BUT ONE TRICK...

BUT YOU KEPT US IN THE ONIWABANSHŪ, AND SO TO YOU...TO THE OKASHIRA... WE GIVE OUR LIVES...

I'M SORRY...

...FOR BEING... IN THE END...SO USE...

...LESS...

TONK

ROLL ROLL

BESHIMI—!!

≡PHEW≡ THAT WAS CLOSE!

THAT FREAK COULD ACTUALLY HAVE HURT ME!

RRGH

YOU... BASTARD!!

...BATTŌSAI.

PNG

HOW LONG TO GRAB THAT SAKABATŌ OF YOURS...

...AND CUT HIM IN TWO?

FIFTEEN... NO.
TEN SECONDS.

READ
THIS
WAY

TEN, HUH?
MIGHT BE TIGHT.
EH?
LOOK.
PNG

UP THOSE STAIRS, THE SECOND FLIGHT. THERE'S A SMALL OBSERVATORY.
TAKANI MEGUMI IS IMPRISONED THERE.

HAN'NYA ...
IT WASN'T THAT I BORE NO THOUGHT FOR THE WOMAN.
IT'S JUST THAT LORD AOSHI CONCERNED ME MORE.
I LEAVE THE REST TO YOU...
HIMURA BATTOSAI.
HAN'NYA, STOP!!
DM

HAN'NYA...
....
!

CHAK

STOP RIGHT THERE, BATTŌSAI!!

JUST LIKE A COLD-BLOODED HITOKIRI TO USE THAT MONSTER AS BAIT.
HAH WAH
HAH HAH
WELL, THEY'VE ALL DIED FOR *NOTHING!*

KENSHIN!!
YOUR TURN!!

SHHHHH
200 SHOTS A MINUTE.
IF YOU KEEP SHOOTING RECKLESSLY...
IT'S OUT OF AMMO!!
?!
USE YOUR HEAD.
SO THEY DID NOT DIE FOR NOTHING.
TM TM TM
A...
A...
AAA...
THE LIVES OF THE FOUR ONIWABANSHŪ...
...HAVE BEATEN YOUR GATLING GUN.
SPARE ME-E-E...
IF YOU'RE GOING TO BEG FOR YOUR LIFE...
...PRAY TO YOUR BELOVED MONEY!!

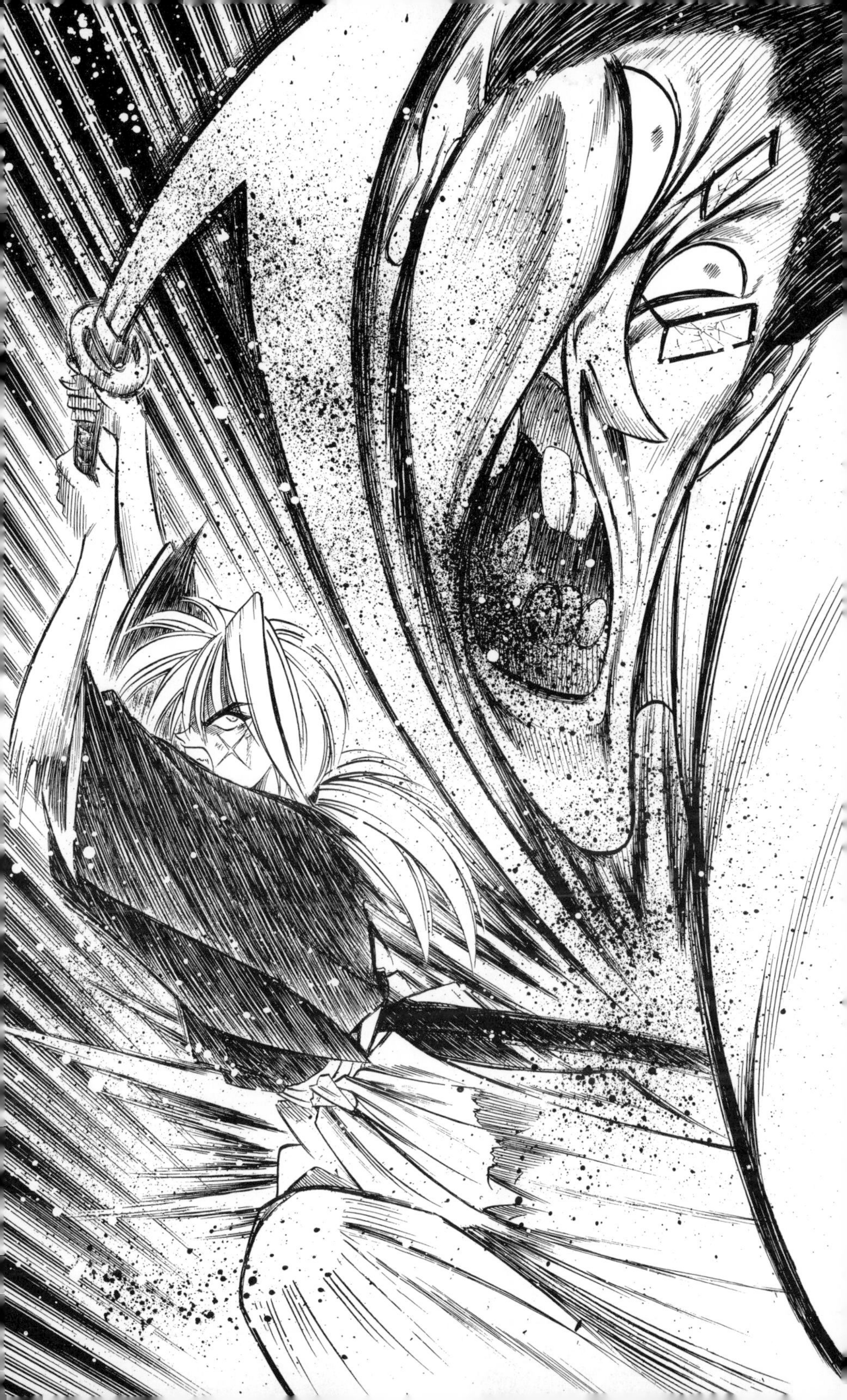

HE'P
...
MEEEE
...
PWEASE
...
SPT
SPT

EVEN IN RAGE, KENSHIN UPHOLDS HIS VOW NOT TO KILL.
...MOSTLY.
POKE
POKE

......

LET'S GO.

MEGUMI-DONO IS WAITING.

The Secret Life of Characters (12)

—Takeda Kanryū—

Just as they did with Sanosuke, Shinsengumi fans will recognize right off that Kanryū is based on the captain of the 5th unit of the Shinsengumi, Takeda Kanryūsai. A man who studied *Kōshū-ryū* war theory, Takeda Kanryūsai was a rare Shinsengumi intellectual. His personality, though, was bad—kissing up to superiors, being mean and sneaky to subordinates. Basically, he was jumping on the Shinsengumi bandwagon, and once the outlook started to turn grim, he tried to defect to Satsuma Prefecture but was found out. He was disciplined...and that was the end of him. The main characters of Shinsengumi novels are almost always the same gang of four: Serizawa Kamo, Yamanami Keisuke, Itō Kashitarō, Takeda Kanryūsai. The first three had their own beliefs and ways of life to provide narrative conflict, but as the "sincere fool," Takeda Kanryūsai had his own narrative value, and so I used him as a model here. I found myself putting so much emphasis on Megumi and the Oniwabanshū, though, that Takeda Kanryū never became the character I wanted him to be. That for me was a bit of a letdown.

Purely as a sidenote, the historical Kanryūsai Takeda is well-known as having been gay, and so of course I thought about that for my own Takeda. On top of it being irrelevant to the plot, though, it was thought that it might unnecessarily complicate things, and so it was dropped. I do wonder sometimes how the story might have gone, had we done it that way.

There is no real model in terms of design. Takeda Kanryū is a carry-over from Nishiwaki in the stand-alone *Rurouni* episodes, and wears white if only because, between Kenshin and Aoshi, there was too much black already. And that's all I have to say about that.

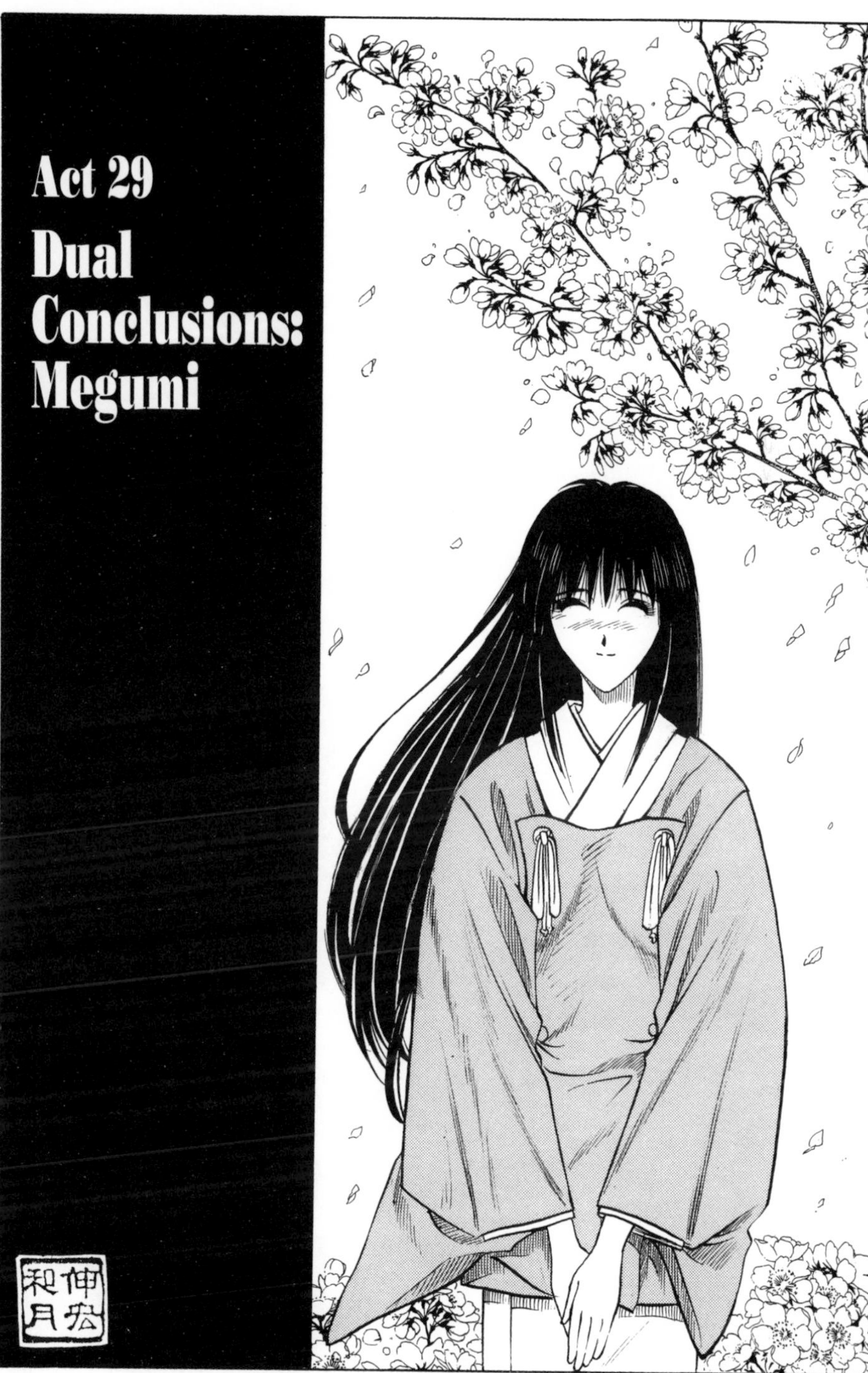
Act 29
Dual Conclusions: Megumi
伸宏
和月

KENSHIN!

LET'S HURRY. MEGUMI-DONO IS WAITING.

HUF

HUF

HUF

HUF

IT'S ALL RIGHT. LITTLE UN-BALANCED, IS ALL.

NOW MORE THAN EVER, I'D SAY.
YEAH.
HMM?

SHINOMORI AOSHI.

YOU'RE QUITE A MAN TO BE ABLE TO WOUND KENSHIN SO BADLY.

BUT THE WOUND YOU RECEIVED IN THIS BATTLE IS MUCH GREATER.

THE GUNSHOTS... STOPPED.

NOW WHAT...?

!

KCH

PWIK

KCH

KCH

KCH

KCH

ARRGH! STUPID DOOR !!

ALL RIGHT!
NO HIDDEN MEN.
TM
YAHIKO...
SANOSUKE...

TM
SORRY TO KEEP YOU WAITING...
MEGUMI-DONO.

KEN-SAN...

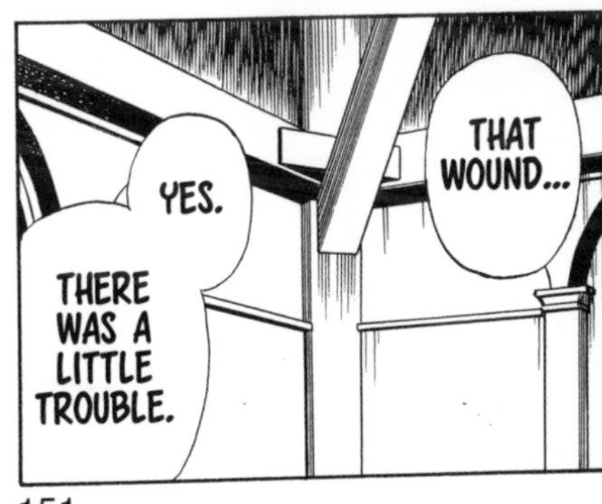
THAT WOUND...
YES.
THERE WAS A LITTLE TROUBLE.

BUT NEVER MIND THAT. WHAT'S IMPORTANT...
IS THAT YOU'RE NOT HURT.

I'M SO SORRY...
I GOT YOU INTO THIS.
I PUT YOU ALL INTO DANGER.
BUT...
SPP
...IT'S ALMOST OVER.

READ THIS WAY

SOON, YOUR WORRIES...
WILL END WITH ME.
!
MEGUMI-DONO!!

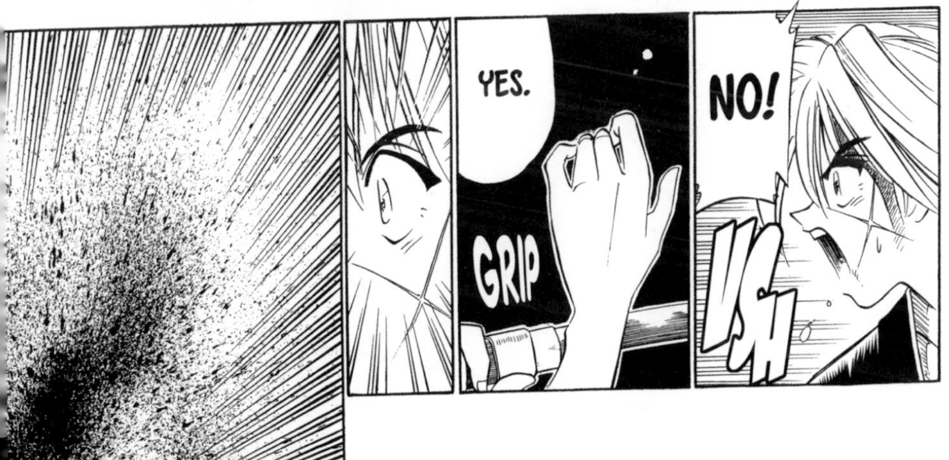

UH?
YOU...
TUG
...STUPID WENCH! KENSHIN AND YAHIKO NEARLY GOT THEMSELVES KILLED TO RESCUE YOU!
AND YOU WANT TO MAKE THAT ALL A WASTE!
GOT IT?!
GRAB
SLUMP
BUT...
...I HAVE NO CHOICE.
PEOPLE ARE SUFFERING FROM MY OPIUM.
HOW CAN I JUST SAY, "THEY FORCED ME..." AND GO ON LIVING?

Here's something I've noticed. I've been getting comments in letters lately along the lines of, "I love the Shinsengumi, too! I hate the Ishin Shishi." Or, "I can't believe you like the Shinsengumi. What are you, an anti-shōgunate dog?" People, in other words, who acknowledge only one side of the conflict. This is a shame, if you ask Watsuki. One of the most interesting things about the Bakumatsu is that there were 100 different factions fighting for 100 different causes. They lived according to their own beliefs, not by some "this side, not that side" mentality. Watsuki's personal favorite may be the Shinsengumi's Hijikata Toshizō, but his second favorite is (pro-Imperialist) Ōkubo Toshimichi. To those of you who've discovered an interest in the Meiji Restoration because of *RuroKen*, keep reading! Keep enjoying! Remember, there wouldn't have *been* a revolution without the Imperialists *and* the Shōgunists. See you next volume!

Watsuki

HEY!

THIS IS BAD, KENSHIN!

GOT 'IM!

IT'S THE POLICE!!

C'MON!

PWEEEEEE

GO! GO!

HEY!

LET'S GO!

THEY MUST HAVE HEARD THE RACKET!!

....

WE GOTTA GET OUT OF HERE!!

DON'T JUST STAND THERE, COME ON! HURRY!!
JERK
!
WHAT TH—
STEP
KEN-SAN...

READ THIS WAY

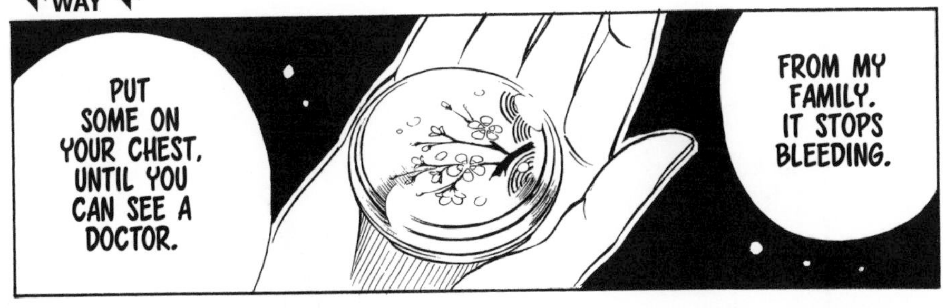
FROM MY FAMILY. IT STOPS BLEEDING.
PUT SOME ON YOUR CHEST, UNTIL YOU CAN SEE A DOCTOR.

KANRYŪ BUILT A SECRET PASSAGE THROUGH THE CEILING...
LEAVE THROUGH THAT, AND YOU CAN ESCAPE.

I'M SO SORRY FOR IT ALL.
TRADING IN OPIUM IS PUNISHABLE BY DEATH.
TWIK

IS THIS WHAT YOU WANT, KNOWING THAT?
MEGUMI-DONO.

...YES.
PEOPLE HAVE DIED, LIKE SANOSUKE'S FRIEND, BECAUSE OF MY OPIUM.
THERE'S NO RUNNING FROM THAT.

THE LIVES I'VE TAKEN WILL BE PAID FOR...

...WITH MY OWN LIFE.

TUP TUP TUP

CHIEF, WE'VE FOUND IT!
A HIDDEN CHAMBER IN THE BASEMENT!!
TM
THEN SECURE IT!
WHOA!
WOW!
AW, NO!!
KEEP QUIET!!
THEY'RE ALL PART OF THE RING!
GET 'IM!
HOLD EVERY LAST ONE!
LET GO!
GOT 'IM!
I ALWAYS HOPED WE'D HAVE A CHANCE TO GET IN HERE...
GLAD IT CAME *SOONER*, RATHER THAN *LATER*.
THOUGH I'D NEVER HAVE EXPECTED A GATLING GUN!
!
TUP

THAT'S HER! THE MAKER OF THE NEW OPIUM!

MY PARTNER IN CRIME!

WHO ARE YOU?

NO ESCAPE FOR *YOU*, MEGUMI! WHATEVER YOU SAY, YOU'RE STILL THE ONE WHO MADE IT!

I'M TAKING YOU WITH ME TO THE BOTTOM OF *HELL*!!

HYAAAAAAA HAHAA

......

IT...

IS THIS TRUE?

SKUP
...IS—
NOT, SIR. ♡
HIMURA-SAN?!
DWAH?!
KWNSWN? (KEN-SAN?)
BLUSH
THIS YOUNG LADY WAS THE PROTÉGÉ OF A GREAT DOCTOR, WHICH IS WHY SHE WAS COERCED INTO MAKING THE OPIUM.
WHAT?!
DON'T LIE, BATTŌSAI!
SHE'S—

YOU BE QUIET.

GLARE

EEE

BATTŌ...SAI?!

RIGHT, YAHIKO?
YES, SIR!
TOKYO SAMURAI MYŌJIN YAHIKO HERE!
WOULD I DEFEND AN OPIUM SMUGGLER? NO SIR, I WOULD NOT!
TA-DAAH

RIGHT, SANO?
DON'T LOOK AT ME. I CAME FOR THE FIGHT.
STILL, IF YOU INSIST ON ARRESTING HER...
...I MAY GET MY SECOND WIND.
KRAK KRAK

SO...

THAT'S HOW IT IS, CHIEF.

.....

NO?

FAIR ENOUGH. IF HIMURA-SAN SAYS IT...

...THEN IT'S THE TRUTH.

GLINT

WHAT?! WHAT THE... WHAT??

THAT WOMAN IS MY ACCOMPLICE! YOU'LL SEE SHE—

WHAT ARE YOU WAITING FOR?! ARREST THIS MAN!

YESSIR!

NOOOO!

NO FAIR!!

SHUT UP AND WALK!

DRAG DRAG

IT'S NOT TOTALLY UNTRUE...

SURE, OKAY, WHATEVER.

KEEP TELLING YOURSELF THAT.

KEN-SAN...
WHY DID YOU...?
"THE LIVES I'VE TAKEN WILL BE PAID FOR WITH MY OWN LIFE."
THAT'S ONE WAY TO LOOK AT IT...
...BUT IT DOESN'T MEAN THEY COME *BACK* ONCE *YOU* DIE.
LIVES CAN ALSO BE PAID FOR BY THE SWORD...
...BY REDEEMING YET *OTHER* LIVES.
THAT IS WHY "HITOKIRI BATTŌSAI"...
...IS STILL ALIVE IN THE MEIJI ERA.

HITOKIRI BATTŌSAI ...!
THE... LEGENDARY ...?

AND MEDICINE LIKE THIS CAN SAVE EVEN MORE THAN BATTŌSAI'S SWORD.
SOOP

BECOME A DOCTOR, MEGUMI-DONO.
FWIK

HELP THOSE SUFFERING NOT JUST FROM OPIUM, BUT FROM ALL PAINS AND ILLS.
KOP

IF YOU DO...I'LL FORGIVE YOU...

...FOR MY FRIEND.

BETCHA RUN INTO YOUR *FAMILY* THAT WAY, TOO!

EEK!

FFWAP

LET'S GO HOME.
KAORU-DONO IS WAITING.
...LET'S!

READ THIS WAY

AH...
CHIEF. ONCE YOU GET TO AOSHI...
AOSHI? WHO IS THAT?

?!
A TALL MAN WEARING A COAT, RIGHT HERE...
?

NO. ONLY KANRYŪ WAS IN THE BALLROOM WHEN WE CAME.

ALONG WITH FOUR BODIES...
...EACH MISSING THEIR HEADS.

The Secret Life of Characters (13)

—Takani Megumi—

There's no real model, but when creating her I imagined a mature woman. Some of you were no doubt surprised to see how different she turned out here as compared to *Rurouni* (Volume 1) but, for me, they both spring from the same spirit and therefore aren't really that unalike.

The stand-alone Megumi did have a lighter quality to begin with, but that was because she didn't have as much to do. Once I realized that she would also appear in this series, I knew she had to make more of an impression and I therefore gave her a more earthy quality. It was my first time with this kind of character, though, and so there was a lot to learn. Looking back now, she isn't nearly what I'd wanted, and that's a bit disappointing. Still, the heart of the drama flows from her deepest inner spirit, and so I suppose that's to be expected.

Megumi was entertaining to draw—and is the one character who can talk "female-to-female" with Kaoru—so I plan to have her appear frequently as a secondary character. She also has the convenience of being a doctor. According to reader mail, two main opinions prevail: (1) "Megumi and Aoshi are suited for each other," and (2) "Megumi and Sano are suited for each other." Watsuki wonders if, in the case of the former, the "suited" part is meant intellectually, while the latter "suited" may be meant temperamentally. Just as with Kenshin and Kaoru, though, at this point I have no such plans for her future. The Megumi arc has "redemption for her crimes" as its theme, and I wanted to express through Megumi Kenshin's determination. (This second part, though, was really tough to pull off.) To write about Kenshin's redemption for his own crimes...thinking of that, I get a headache.

The model in terms of design is the young grandma appearing in Obata-sensei's *Cyborg Ji'i-chan 'G' (Cyborg Grandpa 'G')*. That manga's given me ideas for a long time but, obviously, I can't draw as well as the sensei, and now his character has turned into my own rather lame Megumi. Sigh....

Act 30
Dual Conclusions: Aoshi

AOSHI...
...IS GONE ?!!

NO WINDOWS...

...MEANING, HE WENT OUT A LOWER EXIT.

ARE YOU SURE YOU DON'T NEED NEW GLASSES?!
MAYBE YOU DIDN'T *LOOK* CLOSE ENOUGH.
DON'T BE FOOLISH. EVERY LAST EXIT IS UNDER GUARD BY THE POLICE!
MUSTACHE
NO ONE COULD HAVE COME IN OR OUT OF THE MANSION WITHOUT BEING NOTICED. THE GROUNDS, EITHER.
THEN DID HE REALLY... LIKE AN ONMITSU...
DISAPPEAR INTO SMOKE?

NO SUCH THING.
THERE'S ANOTHER EXIT NO ONE'S MENTIONING.
!

OH!

KANRYŪ'S SECRET PASSAGE !!

IN THE FEW MOMENTS BETWEEN THE TIME KEN-SAN AND THE OTHERS CAME TO THE OBSERVATORY, AND THE POLICE RAIDED THE MANSION...

HE ESCAPED USING THE PASSAGE THROUGH THE ATTIC!

THIS EXIT—WHERE?!
IT GOES DOWN INSIDE THE WALLS FROM THE ATTIC TO THE FOREST BEHIND THE HOUSE.
FOLLOW ME!
D-D-D-D-D

AOSHI...!

HF
HF
HF
HF
THE DOOR'S OPEN.
HE *DID* COME THROUGH HERE...

SEARCH! HE MUST STILL BE CLOSE BY!
YADA
YADA
STOP EVEN A *KITTEN* GOING PAST!

.....
BRRR
WH-WHAT'RE YOU DOING?! ARREST HI—
UH...
NOT SO FAST. YOU'LL ALL JUST BE KILLED.
EH?
STOP.

IT'S NOT YOUR FAULT.

THAT GATLING GUN—WHAT COULD YOU HAVE DONE?

THE ONIWABANSHŪ DIED TO LET YOU LIVE.
BUT THEY WERE HAPPY TO DO IT.

.....

AOSHI.

READ THIS WAY

IF YOU REALLY CANNOT FORGIVE YOURSELF...

...LET US FIGHT, ONE MORE TIME.

!

FIGHT... AND THEN WIN.

TAKE THE TITLE, "MOST POWERFUL"... FOR THOSE FOUR'S GRAVES.

UNTIL I COME KILL YOU...
...DON'T LET ANYONE BEAT ME TO IT.
PFF
TM
!
AFTER HIM! NOW!!
DM
KENSHIN...
HEY!
HEY!
STOP!

SO HE GOES.
NO POINT WORRYING ABOUT IT.
BUT NOW...
...YOU'LL BE A TARGET!
GRIN
IT'S FINE...
...REALLY.

SO.
THIS TIME FOR REAL.
LET'S GO HOME.

WELCOME BACK!!
POP
WE'RE HOME!
YOU GUYS... SO MANY INJURIES...
YOU ALL RIGHT?
SEEMS YOU'VE A FEW YOURSELF, KAORU-DONO...
WELL, WHATEVER THE REASON... GOOD WORK!
BREAK-FAST AND BATHS ARE ALL READY!
ENJOY!

READ THIS WAY

I'M TIRED. I'M GOING TO SLEEP. I'LL USE THE FUTON.
ZIP ZIP
ZIP ZIP
ME, TOO.

BOO HOO
I WORKED SO HARD....
.....
HOO HOO
UM... THIS ONE WOULD LOVE TO...

ME, TOO...
IF IT'S ALL RIGHT.
GRIN
OF COURSE!

AND SO THE STORY OF THE OPIUM RING AND GREAT BATTLE...
OH, IT'S BAD...
BLEH
...
...ENDS WITH DUAL CONCLU-SIONS.

ALSO...
THANK YOU...
...FOR YOUR HOSPITALITY.

I WISH IT WEREN'T SO SMALL HERE, OR THAT THERE WAS SO LITTLE FOOD...
...ESPECIALLY SINCE SOMEONE STILL EATS FOR FREE.
.....
AN ASSISTANT LIKE MEGUMI IS ALWAYS WELCOME.
HEH HEH
HEH HEH
RUB RUB
.....
NO, PLEASE! THANK YOU FOR FINDING ME THE LIVE-IN JOB.
SOMEBODY CALL THE DOCTOR...
UM... KEN-SAN?
ORO?
TWITCH TWITCH
YOU ARE THE DOCTOR!

CALL ME WHEN YOU'RE BORED WITH KAORU-CHAN.
I BET I CAN KEEP YOU... ENTERTAINED.

READ THIS WAY

"ENTER-TAINED"... HOW?

GRRRRR!

ARE YOU GONE YET, YOU *VIXEN* ??!

I'M SO BAD.

LOOK, I TOLD YOU.

SHE'S KINDA SIMPLE. NOT MUCH FOR JOKES.

OH, BUT...

NEITHER AM I.

AND IF I WERE WITH *YOU*, IT *WOULD* BE A JOKE.

HEH HEH

YOU SELLING ME A FIGHT?

FEH. I THOUGHT YOU'D STRAIGHTENED UP A LITTLE WITH ALL THIS.

GUESS NOT.

TCH

SILLY. IT'S FAR TOO LATE AT 22 TO START CHANGING ONE'S WICKED WAYS.

HEH

NO JEALOUSY NOW.
HEH HEH
YOU COULD LEARN A LOT FROM KEN-SAN. MAKE HIM YOUR MODEL.
THEN MAYBE...I'LL ENTERTAIN YOU, TOO.
SPYOO
SEE YA!
KLAK KLAK

TCH
IT'S ALL SOUNDING SO FAMILIAR...
"ENTERTAIN"? HOW "ENTERTAIN"?

WELL, IN ANY EVENT...
AARGH!
...AT LEAST IT'S ALL SETTLED.
NO VIXENS ALLOWED!!
AND DON'T COME BACK!
SHUT UP ALREADY.

FOR MEGUMI-DONO, PERHAPS.

SO BY MAKING YOUR LIFE HIS TARGET...
...YOU GAVE AOSHI A REASON TO LIVE.

READ THIS WAY

NOT TO MENTION ESCAPE THE POLICE PURSUIT AND GO INTO HIDING.
YES... AND HE'LL STAY THAT WAY FOR A WHILE.

HE'LL HEAL HIS WOUNDS, RETRAIN HIMSELF...
UNTIL HE'S CONFIDENT THIS ONE CAN BE DEFEATED.

BEFORE MEGUMI-DONO, THERE WAS NO FEAR.
BUT WHAT OF THE NEXT TIME...?
YEAH, RIGHT!
GNG
KENSHIN NEVER LOSES!
HOPEFULLY NOT.
IN THE MEAN-TIME...

...WOULD THAT EVEN SHINOMORI AOSHI FINDS A PLACE IN THIS WORLD FOR HOPE.

KSSH

HMM?

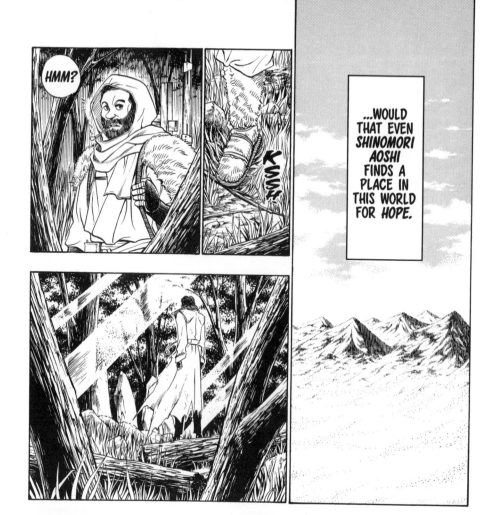

FOR NOW...
...I CAN OFFER YOU NO GLORY.

BUT, ONE DAY...

...I WILL.

HEY, WHAT ARE YOU DOING...

...ALONE DEEP IN THE MOUNTAINS?

VSH

WWIP

TM TM

HEY, DON'T GO THAT WAY!

EVEN THE LOCALS DON'T GO THERE.

NOT EVEN SWORDSMEN OR MARTIAL ARTISTS IN *TRAINING* DO THAT!!

TP-TP TP TP TP

HEY?! DO YOU HEAR ME?!

TM

HEY ...!!!

The Secret Life of Characters (14)

—Okashira • Shinomori Aoshi—

As mentioned previously in regard to Beshimi, the Oniwabanshū were tacked on at the last minute, and so when it was time for Aoshi to appear, I hadn't really worked out a concrete image and therefore had some trouble writing him. With time, though, the models for the Oniwabanshū became my favorite Shinsengumi, and Aoshi's model became the Assistant Chief of the Shinsengumi, Hijikata Toshizō. Even citing Hijikata as a reference, though, there's still two versions of him in the novels (you Shinsengumi hardcores know what I'm talking about).

One Hijikata is the one from *Moeyo Ken (Burn, O Sword)*, a bundle of raw combat instinct who keeps fighting until the very death. (It's this Hijikata that Watsuki is a fan of.) The other Hijikata is the one who hides his selfishness for the sake of the Shinsengumi, acting mercilessly but crying inside. (That's the one Aoshi has as his model.) "The Shinsengumi who could not fight..." In other words, they couldn't show their beliefs, honor, or abilities to the outside world, and so were labeled the defeated. The Asst. Chief who fought to keep his Oniwabanshū from hiding their lights beneath a bushel, that's Aoshi. I won't reveal here whether or not Aoshi will become an ogre-like warrior who fights to the death, but his reappearance isn't that far away.

There's no specific design model for him. I first used a character I have in my sketchbook, but as the story went on, the image of Hijikata became stronger and stronger, causing me to add the bangs. When editing the (compiled) manga, I had the chance to change it, but that might seem kind of strange, so I let it be—I wouldn't want anyone to think Aoshi was wearing a rug or anything.

Rurouni
Kenshin

Rurouni Kenshin

VOLUME 5: The State of Meiji Swordsmanship

Act 31
Bonus Story: Yahiko's Battle (1)

YAHIKO!!!

MMMG!

YAHIKO! YAHIKO!!!

WHAT'S THE BIG IDEA WITH THAT HAIRSTYLE?!
WHERE DO YOU GET OFF INSULTING MY HAIR?!
I'LL BELT YOU!
I'LL KICK YOU!
WHAT'S ALL THAT RACKET?
...YAHIKO'S GONE?
YOU HEARD ME!
NOW THAT YOU MENTION IT... HE HAS BEEN DISAPPEARING A LOT LATELY.
SURE HAS!
SCRUB
SCRUB
MAYBE HE FOUND A GIRL.
KID'S CLEVER THAT WAY.
PROBABLY HE'S OUT SCROUNG-ING FOR FOOD.
HE EATS LIKE HE'S TWICE HIS SIZE.
ANOTHER GUESS WOULD BE TRAINING ON HIS OWN.
NO DOUBT HE'D LIKE TO PUT WHAT HE'S LEARNED TO THE TEST.
SCRUB
SCRUB

NOT A CHANCE !!

WE THINK.

YES, BUT...

HMPH!

A GIRL, A GIRL! WHAT ELSE?

FOOD! I'M SURE IT'S FOOD!

BLAH

THIS ONE THINKS *SWORDS*...

IT CAN'T BE!

BLAH

IT'S FOOD...

...A GIRL...

TKTK

TKTK

FOOD? GIRLS? IS *THIS* WHAT YOU TALK ABOUT WHEN I'M NOT AROUND?

YOU GUYS ARE SAD.

PWHI

KABLAM

YOU BRAT!!!!!

RRRG!
GIMME A BREAK!
ROAR
WHAT IS YOUR PROBLEM?!

SO WHERE WERE YOU, YAHIKO?
FWAP
FWAP
SKRIK
JUST A WALK.
A WALK WHEN YOU SHOULD BE TRAINING...
THAT'S NOT "JUST" A WALK.
HEH
RK...

A FEW DAYS LATER...

谷活心流
剣術道場

KLATTA

TM

READ
THIS
WAY

GLANCE
...GOOD.
GLANCE
NOBODY'S FOLLOWING ME...

....
KENSHIN'S ONTO ME.
BETTER BE CAREFUL.
TATATATATA
TATATATATA

...OKAY. MAYBE YOU'RE RIGHT.
HE'S HIDING SOMETHING.
IT GIVES US SOME-THING TO DO, ANYWAY.

BETCHA ANYTHING IT'S A GIRL.
TPTPTP
FORGET IT. FOOD.
TPTPTP
WHY WON'T ANYONE CONSIDER SWORDS...?
TPTPTPTPTP

BEEF BOWL SHOP "AKABEKO"...
THAT'S WHERE I ALWAYS EAT!
EASY TO SKIP OUT OF...
酒処 牛鍋 赤べこ
牛鍋

SEE, I KNEW IT WAS FOOD!!
GNG
TOLDJA SO...
ORO?
PEH.

IF HE THINKS HE CAN GET AWAY WITH...
KLATAT
...THIS...
HUH?

READ THIS WAY

Long time no see, indeed. Watsuki here. The third volume of the CD books has been decided on: the "Jin-e" episodes. At the time I'm writing this, it's just been decided, so I have no information about the script or the voice actors. The script probably will be based pretty closely on the original story, with a little massaging to increase the appearances of Sanosuke and Yahiko. For the voice actor, I'd like someone with a mature but cool voice. In my mind, Jin-e is a mad hero, so I'd like to avoid an actor with a high voice...basically, though, I'm leaving it to Jump Media Mix and Fukui-san. I didn't expect it to get so far...and it's all because of you readers. Recently, I've been given a really tough schedule, and honestly speaking, I've had some times when I've wanted to quit writing. But it's too early to "give up" on manga. As long as there are people who read, support, and anticipate, I will have to write, and will want to write. I'm going to keep working on *Ruroken*, keeping my original goals in mind.

Watsuki

HEY, KID!
WE'RE RUNNING LOW ON CHARCOAL. BRING US ANOTHER SACK!
ZIP
YES, SIR!
TSUBAME, YOU GO GET ONE, TOO.
AND IT'S STARTING TO FILL UP INSIDE, SO GO HELP OUT!
Y—YES SIR...
I SEE. HE RUNS ERRANDS IN THE BACK.
YES. I'VE BEEN ASKED NOT TO TELL.
POING POING
HE JUST SHOWED UP...
...AND ASKED FOR A JOB. ON THE QUIET.
SNEEEEK

BUT WHY IS HE DOING THIS...?

MAYBE *THAT'S* YOUR ANSWER.

SPLAT

"THAT" ...?

MRRK
OH, TSUBAME?
I DON'T THINK SO. SHE CAME TO US AFTER YAHIKO DID.

WHAT ARE YOU DOING? HURRY UP!
I-I'M SORRY...
YAHIKO-CHAN.

NN
I TOLD YOU NOT TO CALL ME "*CHAN*"!!
SORRY! SORRY!
TWIK

BRR

AND DON'T GET SO SCARED ALL THE TIME!
GRAB
I HATE IT WHEN PEOPLE ACT THAT WAY.
OH...

YAHIKO-CHA...
YAHIKO-KUN.
WORKING THE LEGS AND WAIST IS PART OF A SWORDS-MAN'S TRAINING.
WOBBLE
WOBBLE
DON'T MIND ME, JUST GO BACK AND HELP.
.....

FOOD, GIRL, AND SWORDS.
ALL OF US WERE RIGHT!

BUT NONE OF THEM SEEM TO BE WHAT HE'S AFTER...

COULD HE JUST BE LOOKING FOR SOME SPENDING MONEY?

YADA

THEN WHY WOULD HE HAVE TO KEEP IT A SECRET?

HMM...

YADA

YADA

YADA

COULD IT BE HE'S TRYING TO SUPPLEMENT THE DOJO'S BUDGET?
YEAH, RIGHT.
KID'S NOT THAT GENEROUS.
HMPH.
LOOK WHO'S TALKING!
MOOCHER.

HEY!
I'M TRYIN' TO ORDER, HERE!!
商売繁盛
OH.

SLAPPA
SLAP
C-COMING, SIR.
ZIP
SO SORRY FOR THE WAIT. WHAT WOULD YOU...?

HENH
HEY...

READ THIS WAY

HEH-HEH...

AH...

HOO-HOO...

WHAT'S WITH THE MOPEY FACE?

YOU GIVE THAT LOOK TO YOUR *MASTER?*

GLARE

PHEW.

I'M BEAT!

THIS IS HARDER THAN *KAORU'S* TRAINING!

BUT TO GET MY HANDS ON IT...

I CAN DEAL WITH ANYTHING.

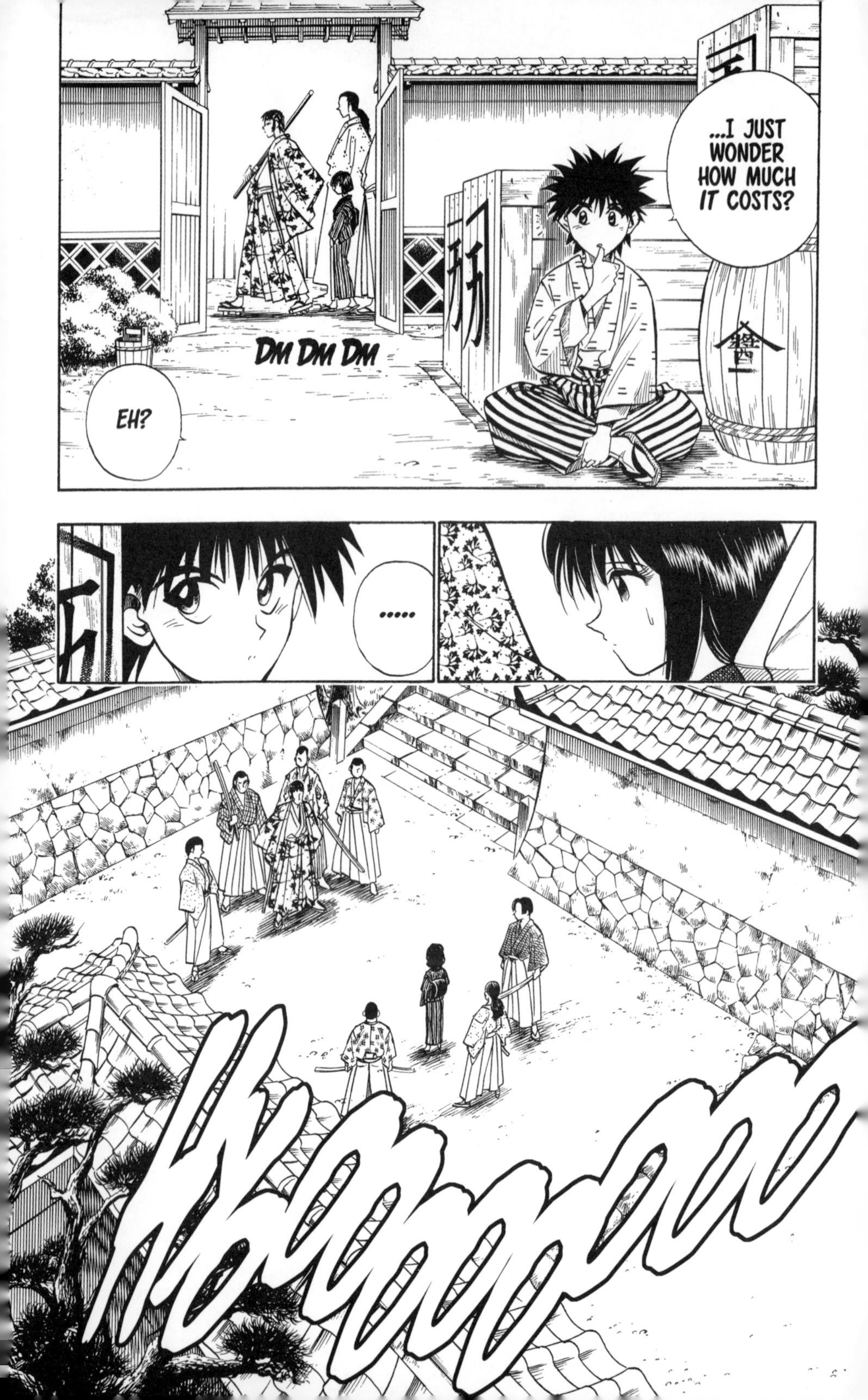

...I JUST WONDER HOW MUCH IT COSTS?

DM DM DM

EH?

......

READ THIS WAY

SO.
WHAT'S THE DEAL?
......
I SAID, WHAT'S THE DEAL?
A...AKABEKO DOESN'T KEEP MUCH CASH THERE.
HE TAKES THE MONEY TO HIS HOUSE EVERY DAY...

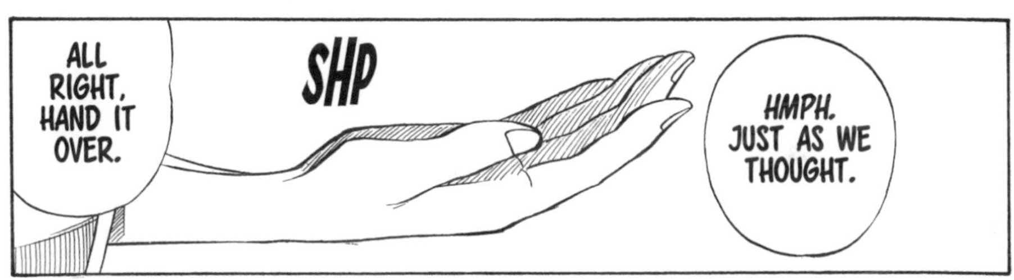
HMPH. JUST AS WE THOUGHT.
SHP
ALL RIGHT, HAND IT OVER.

YOU BROUGHT IT LIKE I TOLD YOU TO, RIGHT?
HENH
THE MOLD FOR THE OWNER'S HOUSE KEY?!

WE...WE SHOULDN'T DO THIS, MIKIO-SAMA!
BURGLARY WILL SHAME THE NAME OF THE NAGAOKA FAMILY...!!
HUH...
AND SINCE WHEN DO *YOU* MATTER ENOUGH TO GIVE ME OPINIONS?!
!
YOU ARE OF A SAMURAI FAMILY! A POOR FAMILY THAT SERVED THE NAGAOKA FOR 300 YEARS!!!
YOU GREW UP WATCHING YOUR FATHER LIVE BY SERVING MINE!
BUT SINCE THE REVOLUTION, NOW THAT THERE *ARE* NO SAMURAI...
...IS MY FAMILY SUDDENLY *NOTHING* TO YOURS?!

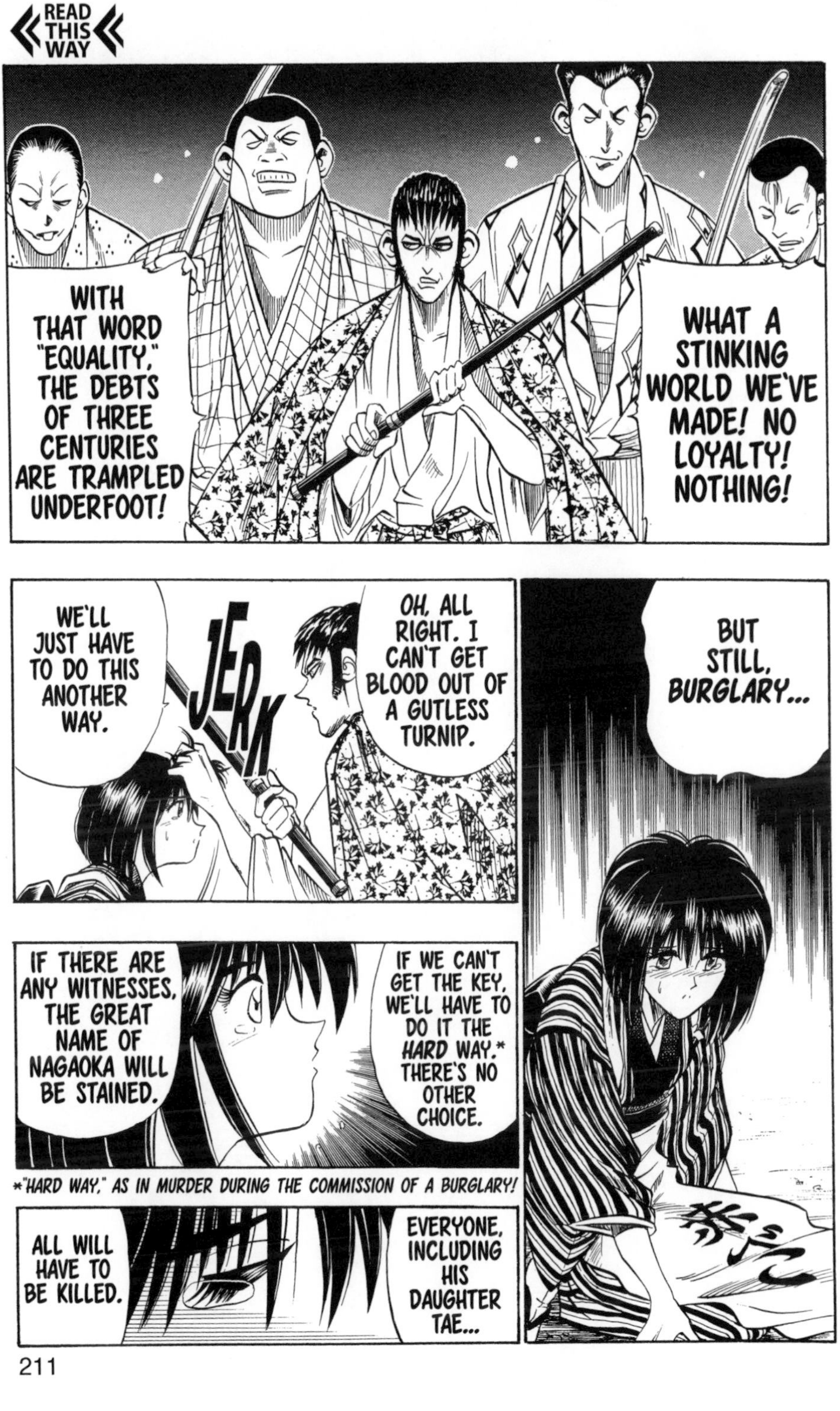

WHAT A STINKING WORLD WE'VE MADE! NO LOYALTY! NOTHING!
WITH THAT WORD "EQUALITY," THE DEBTS OF THREE CENTURIES ARE TRAMPLED UNDERFOOT!

BUT STILL, *BURGLARY*...

OH, ALL RIGHT. I CAN'T GET BLOOD OUT OF A GUTLESS TURNIP.

JERK

WE'LL JUST HAVE TO DO THIS ANOTHER WAY.

IF WE CAN'T GET THE KEY, WE'LL HAVE TO DO IT THE *HARD WAY.** THERE'S NO OTHER CHOICE.

IF THERE ARE ANY WITNESSES, THE GREAT NAME OF NAGAOKA WILL BE STAINED.

*"HARD WAY," AS IN MURDER DURING THE COMMISSION OF A BURGLARY!

EVERYONE, INCLUDING HIS DAUGHTER TAE...

ALL WILL HAVE TO BE KILLED.

.....
ZOOP
HEH, THAT'S A GOOD GIRL.
DON'T WORRY. WE WON'T GET CAUGHT.
HENH
ARE YOU STUPID?!
IT'S BEEN THE MEIJI ERA FOR TEN YEARS! THERE ARE NO "SAMURAI DEBTS" ANYMORE!
GASP
!
WHA...
WHO IS IT?!
TOOM

YOU! SIDE-BURNS!

AS A SAMURAI MYSELF, I WON'T JUST *LET* YOU DO THIS!!

YA... YAHIKO-CHAN!!

DMM

NNN

I TOLD YOU NOT TO CALL ME "*CHAN*"!

Rurouni
Kenshin

Act 32

Bonus Story: Yahiko's Battle (2)

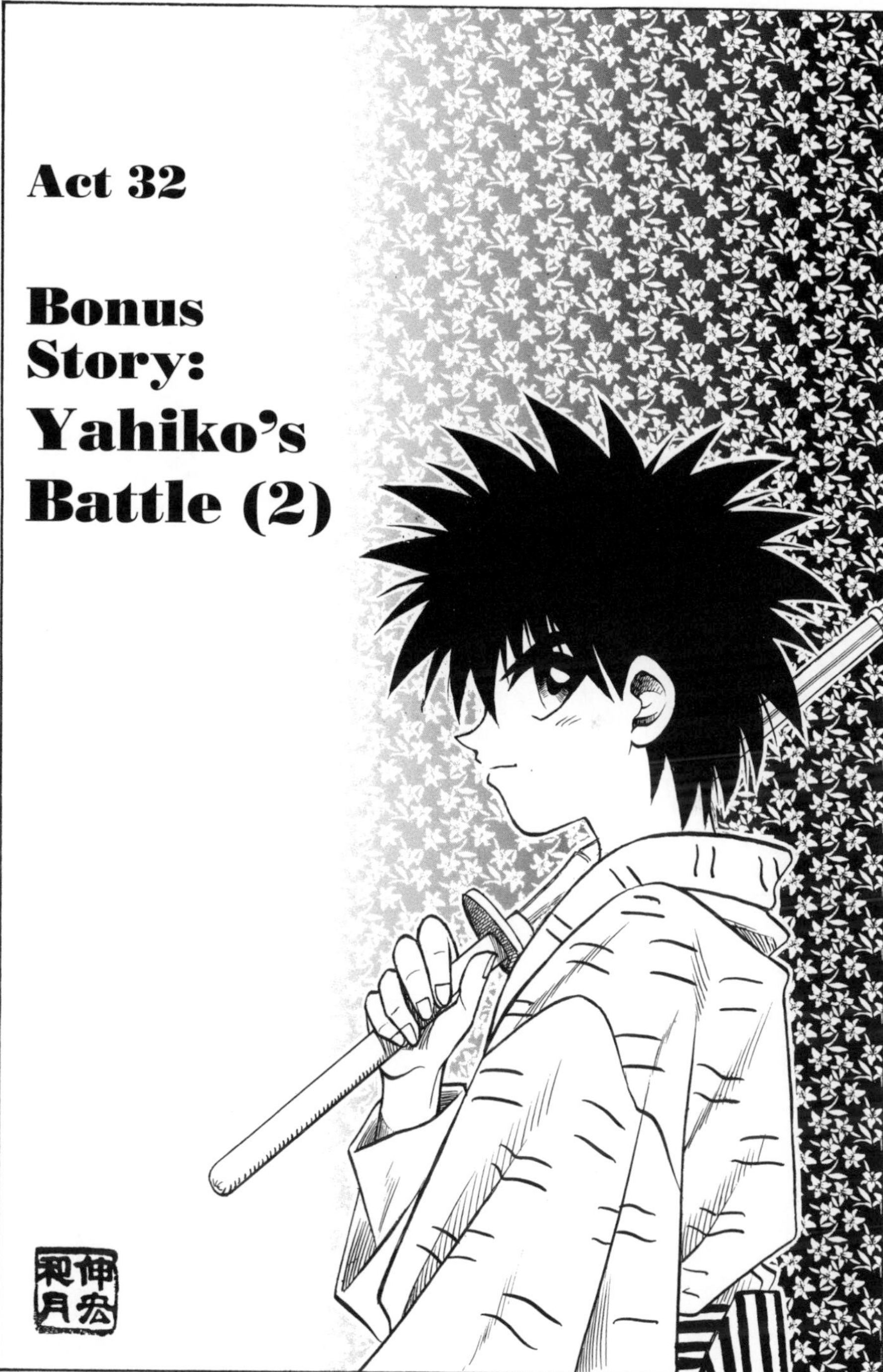

TOH !!!
!!
"TOH"?

PING
PING
PING
PING
YAHIKO-CHAN!!
THROBBBBBBBBB

NOT "CHAN." NOT "CHAN"—!!
RIGHT... SORRY.
ARGH!

HEY.
!
TM

DROP THIS STUPID "BURGLARY" IDEA!
OR ELSE I, MYŌJIN YAHIKO, TOKYO SAMURAI, WILL STAND BEFORE YOU!!
YOU PUNK!!
OH, SHUT UP...
?!

READ THIS WAY
WH...
CHEST!!
DO
WHUH!!
YOU—!!
BM
BM
FACE!!

WOBBLE
...GUH...
IT WORKS!
MY SWORD ACTUALLY BEAT THEM!!

?!
DON'T GET CARRIED AWAY!!
GG
WHA—?

NOW, SURROUND HIM AND FINISH HIM!!
BOK
WAK
THUK
BISH
ZAK
FWOK
TOOM
!

HMPH.
KEEN
NOT EVEN WORTH MY EFFORT.
.....

ORO?
WHADDYA MEAN, "....."
BOOT.
WHY ARE WE HERE JUST WATCHING, AGAIN?

CALM DOWN.
SHAKE
SHAKE
SHAKE
SHAKE
YEAH, YAHIKO'S IN TROUBLE!
HOW CAN I BE CALM?!
EVEN IF HE IS A BIG BRAT, HE'S MY FIRST STUDENT!
VM
HOLD IT.
NN.
KRAK

READ
THIS
WAY

YAHIKO DOESN'T KNOW WE'RE HERE.
HOW DO WE EXPLAIN SUDDENLY SHOWING UP?
BUT—!

BESIDES...
...IF ONE IS ALWAYS BEING HELPED, HOW DOES ONE EVER IMPROVE?

THIS IS YAHIKO'S BATTLE.
IT WOULD BE DIFFERENT IF HE ASKED FOR HELP...
BUT HIS AFFAIRS ARE NOT OURS TO MEDDLE IN.

"LIONS DROP THEIR YOUNG DOWN A CLIFF," SAYS THE PROVERB.
EVEN SO...

STOP... PLEASE STOP!
MIKIO-SAMA!!
GOP
DSH
GOK
KOT
GUG
BOK
BOK
THE BOY HAS NOTHING TO DO WITH THIS!
JUST TAKE THE KEY MOLD... PLEASE!!
DOM
GOM
GRAB
FEH!
ZZM
ZZM
IF...IF IT HAD BEEN ONE-ON-ONE, I...
WE HAVE BIGGER FISH TO FRY.
THAT'S ENOUGH.
YES.
T-T-T-T-
ARE YOU ALL RIGHT?
TSUBAME!

READ THIS WAY

JUST KEEP ON DOING WHAT I TELL YOU.

HENH

BE SEEIN' YA...

HEE HEE HEE

HYAHAHA!

...YAHIKO-CHAN.

I'M SORRY...
IT'S MY FAULT YOU'RE IN THIS...

I'M SO SORRY...

IT TAKES AT LEAST A DAY TO MAKE A GOOD KEY OFF OF A MOLD.
THEY'LL PROBABLY STRIKE TOMORROW NIGHT OR LATER.
YAHIKO-CHAN?!
HOOF

TWIK
OH...

WHAT-EVER.

IF I CAN'T EVEN TAKE ON THOSE BUMS...
...I GUESS I *DESERVE* TO BE CALLED "CHAN."

ANYWAY, YOU DIDN'T PULL ME INTO THIS. I STUCK MY NECK INTO IT ALL ON MY OWN.
IT'S NOT SOMETHING YOU NEED WORRY ABOUT.
SHMP
SHMP

YAHIKO-CHAN...

I CAN'T TELL THE POLICE, 'CAUSE THEN SHE'LL END UP AN ACCOMPLICE.
AND I CAN'T DEPEND ON KENSHIN AND THE OTHERS. BESIDES, THEY AREN'T WORTH KENSHIN'S TIME.
ZUFF
ZUFF
THIS IS *MY* BATTLE!!
......
THE NEXT MORNING ...
CHEE CHEE CHEE
WELL...
I GUESS THIS IS GOOD ENOUGH.

WHAT KIND OF TOY IS THAT?
STUPID !!
I DESIGNED THIS MYSELF, SO THAT I CAN FIGHT MULTIPLE OPPONENTS AT ONCE!
IT'S AN AUTOMATIC TRAINING MACHINE!

HOW DUMB.
AND USELESS!
WHAT DID YOU SAY ?!!

THINK ABOUT IT.
THOSE BOARDS ONLY MOVE IN CERTAIN WAYS, BUT SWORDSMEN STRIKE ALL OVER THE PLACE.
COMBINATIONS, WAVES, ENCIRCLEMENTS. THOSE ARE ONLY A FEW OF THE TRICKS THEY'LL PULL.
JUST LIKE A KID.
AND IT'LL TAKE YOU TOO LONG TO IMPROVE YOURSELF ANYWAY.
RRRG
NN...

READ THIS WAY

YOU TALK LIKE YOU KNOW EVERYTHING! WHAT'S A BETTER WAY, THEN?!
PING
UH.
GULP
W... WELL...
WELL?

MASTERING HITEN MITSURUGI-RYŪ!
HOW'S THAT?
PING
OH, AND THAT'S EASY, ISN'T IT?!

WHAT A USELESS TEACHER.
WHAT DID YOU SAY, SHORTY?!!

SO! KENSHIN! HEY!
LEMME AT 'IM!
ORO?
CAN YOU THINK OF ANYTHING?
A WAY TO FIGHT MULTIPLE OPPONENTS AT ONCE?

THIS ONE WON'T TEACH HITEN MITSURUGI-RYŪ.
SATSUJIN-KEN'S NO GOOD EITHER.
FWAF
SOMETHING I CAN DO IN A DAY, OKAY?!
YOU'RE NOT EVEN LISTENING.

YOU'RE NOT IN...SOME KIND OF SITUATION, ARE YOU?
!
NOTHING LIKE THAT.
I JUST WANT TO KNOW.
...IS THAT SO?

I DO HAVE ONE SUGGESTION.
YEAH?!
IT'S A METHOD USED BY THE ISHIN SHISHI DURING THE BAKUMATSU, WHEN THEY WERE SEVERELY OUTNUMBERED. FIRST, THEY'D RUN...
RUN?
WELL, TO BE EXACT, THEY PRETENDED TO RUN.

THEIR OPPONENTS WOULD START CHASING, OF COURSE, BUT THE FASTER ONES WOULD CATCH UP TO THEM FIRST.
TAKING ADVANTAGE OF THAT, THE PATRIOTS WOULD TURN AND TAKE ONE DOWN, THEN RUN AGAIN.
IF YOU KEEP THAT UP, YOU CAN TAKE DOWN ALL YOUR ENEMIES...OR AT LEAST, GET AWAY.

I SEE!!
PAM
OF COURSE, THAT MEANS BEING A FAST RUNNER...
OH, YEAH...
TCH

THE POINT IS, NO MATTER HOW MANY YOUR OPPONENTS, YOU *HAVE* TO CREATE A SITUATION WHERE IT'S ONE-ON-ONE.
THAT'S WHAT YOU NEED TO THINK ABOUT.
A SITUATION...
...TO FIGHT ONE-ON-ONE.
AND YAHIKO.
HUH?

KAMIYA KASSHIN-RYŪ IS KATSUJIN-KEN...
A SWORD YOU WIELD FOR THE PEOPLE, TO *PROTECT* THE PEOPLE.

YOU CARRY THE TWO FATES, YOURS AND THE ONE YOU PROTECT, ON ONE SWORD.

WHEN YOU LOSE WITH KATSUJIN-KEN, THOSE FATES—YOURS AND THE ONE YOU'RE PROTECTING—WILL BE CLOSED.

HE WHO WIELDS KATSUJIN-KEN IS NOT ALLOWED TO LOSE.

KEEP THAT IN YOUR HEART.

ON MY SWORD...
...I CARRY THE FATE OF THE ONE I AM PROTECTING.
DEFEAT...
...IS NOT AN OPTION.
KAMIYA KASSHIN-RYŪ...
HSS
I, MYŌJIN YAHIKO...
...WILL DO YOU HONOR...
...IN COMBAT!!
DM

Rurouni
Kenshin

Act 33 Bonus Story: Yahiko's Battle (3)

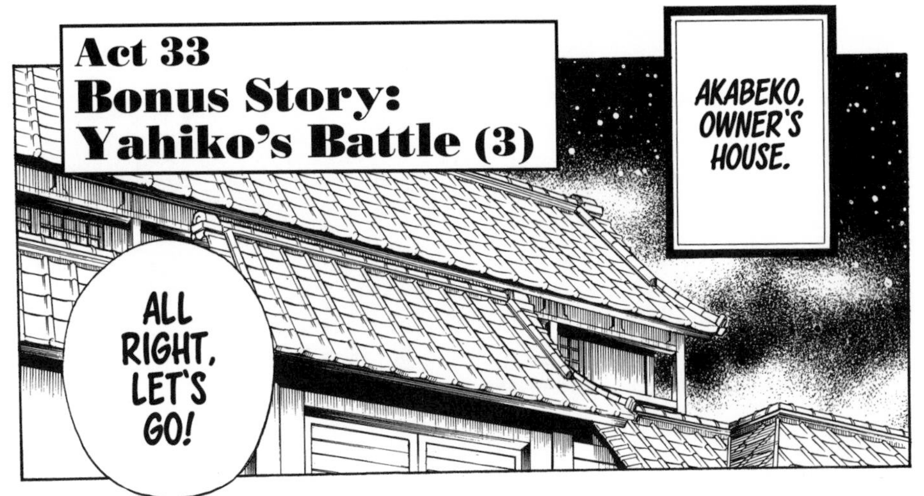

AKABEKO, OWNER'S HOUSE.
ALL RIGHT, LET'S GO!

WE REALLY GOING TO DO THIS, MIKIO-SAN?
EH?
YOU GETTING SCARED NOW?

I TOLD YOU. THESE MERCHANTS WOULDN'T *HAVE* ANY MONEY IF NOT FOR THE SAMURAI.
SO DON'T WE DESERVE TO TAKE IT?
HENH
DON'T WORRY, WE WON'T FAIL.
JINGLE
WE'VE EVEN GOT A KEY, THANKS TO THAT STUPID GIRL...
HYOOO
!

Act 33
Bonus Story: Yahiko's Battle (3)
DM
!!
伸宏
和月

READ THIS WAY

YOU—FROM YESTERDAY...!!
GASP
PICK-POCKET SAVES THE DAY... AGAIN.
BUT IS THAT A GOOD THING?
JINGLE

HYAH
GIVE IT BACK, SHRIMP!!
COME AND GET IT IF YOU WANT IT.
STEALING'S WHAT YOU DO, RIGHT?
VSH
STOP!!

YAHIKO-CHAN...!

DDDDDDD
DONG
WE GOT YOU NOW!
SAY YOUR PRAYERS!!
ALL RIGHT!
COME AT ME!!
THIS TIME, I'M *NOT* GOING TO LOSE!!
SHAH

Seems I'll finally have a chance to get to those fan letters. Just a little while longer, please! I haven't even had time to read the letters recently—and that's not something I'm proud of—but I do plan to make time and read them all. Reading them gives me energy, as usual; some even make me want to say to their authors, "Whoa, whoa, take it easy, huh?" (Even those letters put a smile on my face, though.)

和月伸宏

OHH?!

RRRG!!

GUNG

.....

!
I SEE...HE PRETENDED TO BE BLOCKED IN, BUT WAS REALLY SETTING US UP IN THIS NARROW PLACE TO FIGHT ONE-ON-ONE...
HENH
HMM... GOOD THINKING, FOR A KID.
HE'S FIGURED IT OUT...
TOO BAD THAT WILL MEAN YOUR DEATH!!
YOU HAVE NO PLACE TO RUN!!

WHAT ARE YOU DOGS AFRAID OF?!
NOBODY WILL KNOW WE KILLED A KID OR TWO, NOT IF WE BURY THE BODIES!
BUT THAT'LL KILL HIM...
WHO CARES?!
ALL TOGETHER— THROW YOUR WOODEN SWORDS!

NNN
.....
HN HAH

A-A—AAAAAA?!?!

TH-THAT CROSS-SHAPED SCAR ON HIS CHEEK! IT'S...IT'S HIM!
AND THE OTHER ONE'S ZANZA THE FIGHT MERCHANT!
RUN—OR IT'S OUR BODIES THEY'LL BE BURYING!!
DUM
DUM
DUM
?!

.....!

HEY, WAIT!
WHAT ARE YOU RUNNING FROM?!
YEEE!
THIS IS ABOUT ALL WE CAN DO FOR NOW.
I'M AFRAID SO.

BUT HOW COULD YOU HAVE KNOWN THAT THIS ONE...?
NO ONE ELSE WAS TOLD.

OF COURSE I KNEW.
THIS MAY BE "YAHIKO'S BATTLE," BUT IT'LL BE TSUBAME AND AKABEKO WHO'LL SUFFER IF HE LOSES.

YOU CAN'T LEAVE INNOCENTS IN DANGER.
ANYWAY, YOU'RE TOO DAMN NICE TO JUST LET HIM SINK OR SWIM.
IS THAT A COMPLIMENT, OR AN INSULT...?

EITHER WAY, FROM HERE ON IN...
YES. A TRUE ONE-ON-ONE.

THIS IS WHY STREET PUNKS ARE USELESS!!
JUST WHEN YOU NEED THEM MOST, THEY RUN!
KEEN
NEVER THOUGHT I'D BE USING...
...MY KŌGEN ITTŌ-RYŪ ON A KID.
VSH
BUT HERE IT COMES!!

READ THIS WAY

Hyoo

ORAH!!

!

.....

I SEE IT!!
HH
I CAN SEE THE SWING OF A REAL SWORDS-MAN!
NNNN!!
THE TRAINING'S WORKING!! IT IS!!

GUESS I MAY EVEN HAVE TO THANK KAORU...
DAMN ...!

YOU PUNK!!

......

IT'S DANGEROUS FOR A GIRL TO BE WALKING ALONE THIS LATE AT NIGHT.

PAT

?!

WH- WHO...?

KAMIYA KAORU.

I'M YAHIKO'S TEACHER.

WHEN HE LETS ME.

SO YOU CAME TO STOP HIM.

......

NOD

I HAVE ALWAYS BEEN TAUGHT THAT THE WAY OF A SAMURAI FAMILY WAS TO *SERVE* THE FAMILY OF THE MASTER.
...
...
BUT I CAN'T LET OTHERS SUFFER FOR IT.
SO I CAME TO TRY TO STOP HIM... AND THEN I SAW YAHIKO-CHAN...

TP
YOU'D NEVER BE ABLE TO STOP THAT MAN.
LET YAHIKO HANDLE THIS. BUT PROMISE ME ONE THING.
PROMISE ...?

THAT IF YAHIKO WINS, YOU'LL HAVE A STRONGER HEART!!

!

THAT YOU WON'T BE OWNED BY STINKY OLD CUSTOMS...

AND IF YOU'RE TOLD TO DO ANYTHING LIKE THIS AGAIN, YOU'LL REFUSE!

IT'S NOT ENOUGH FOR THE LAW TO SAY WE'RE ALL EQUAL.
IF PEOPLE'S HEARTS DON'T CHANGE, NONE OF IT MEANS ANYTHING.
DAMNED URCHIN! I'VE HAD ENOUGH OF THIS!!
NOW!!
!!
"FLOATING FOOT-DROP"!!
KŌGEN ITTŌ-RYŪ!
UNH...MY RIGHT FOOT...

WIN!!
PLEASE WIN!
YOU HAVE TO!!
YES! THE "FATE OF THE PROTECTED"...
!
HYOHHHH!!
HE BROKE HIS WEAPON!
OOO.
WHA—?!
I...
...IT RESTS ON MY SWORD !!

...WILL...
WIN!!

HF
HF
HF
...UH?
KAORU! WHAT ARE YOU DOING HERE?
HUH?
OH!
UH...
EEEP
AND YOU TWO—ON THE ROOF!!
.....
CRICK-CRICK CRICKET! CRICKET!!
THERE ARE NO CICADAS IN SPRING!
WHAT KINDA FOOL D'YOU...?
FOOEY...
NEVER KNOW WHEN TO LEAVE A GUY ALONE.

I'LL WALK TSUBAME, SO YOU GO HOME FIRST.
ALL RIGHT. BE CAREFUL.
YAHIKO-KUN... THANK YOU SO MUCH.
DON'T THANK ME. PEOPLE ALL SCARED AND JUMPY LIKE YOU...I JUST CAN'T STAND TO SEE IT.

I WON'T BE LIKE THAT ANYMORE.
I KNOW.

SEE YOU TOMORROW ...
AT AKABEKO.
THE STORY'S OVER...
NO, NOT YET.
WE STILL DON'T KNOW WHY THE KID TOOK THE JOB IN THE FIRST PLACE!
YOIKS!
JAB

READ THIS WAY

AND IF YOU TRY AND TELL ME AFTER ALL THIS THAT IT'S A *SECRET*...
NNNNNN
OKAY, OKAY, I'LL TELL YOU.
IT'S TO BUY A REVERSE-BLADE SWORD.
WHEN I'M AS GOOD AS KENSHIN, I WANT TO HAVE ONE JUST LIKE HIM.
SO I'M SAVING UP.

DAA HA HA HA HA HA!!!
NOW THAT'S A GOOD ONE!
YAHIKO WANTS A SAKABATŌ??!
SANO
!!

DON'T *LAUGH*, BIRDHEAD!!
THIS IS WHY I DIDN'T TELL!!

I'M NOT TELLING *KAORU*, THAT'S FOR SURE!
HOO-HOO-HOO
I ALREADY HEARD.
AS HE'LL SOON LEARN.
I'M NEVER, *EVER* TELLING *HER!*
?

The Secret Life of Characters (15)

—Sanjō Tsubame—

In terms of personality, there's no real model. Created more as a bridge to the "Raijūta" episodes, the main point of the "side story" in this volume was to shine the spotlight on Yahiko—"a young girl being a young man's motivation to act" was the weird thought I found myself having—and thus was the story crafted to provide an opportunity for Tsubame to appear as its heroine. Some cling to their beliefs because of pride or conviction; some because they're just too weak-willed to change. Tsubame's character is testament to the wrong thinking of a previous age...that, and as a direct contrast to "acts-before-he-thinks" Yahiko.

As mentioned above, the Yahiko side story was meant mainly as a bridge and yet, once begun, it also raised all sorts of problems. There was the possibility that it could go longer than three episodes...the desire to focus more on Kenshin and the others...the rapid shuttling back and forth of the action. It was a really tiring story to tell! It was all worth it in the end, though, since the readers liked it, and even though it was short, it managed to successfully capture the world of *RuroKen*. On the other hand, psychological fatigue-wise, the stress of it would drag behind me long after...

In terms of design, you could say the model came from a certain wildly popular "planet-themed" anime show—from the character symbolized by a "ringed planet" in particular. Tsubame's just an average girl, so her hair had to be either a bowl-cut, or in pigtails. While working on a draft of a draft, I chanced to see the show and decided "Right! A bowl-cut it is!" (Why I'd say "Right!" to myself, I've no idea.)

Watsuki doesn't make a habit of watching this kind of anime, mind you, but during his period of apprenticeship, it was suggested to him by the sensei's chief assistant that he do so, and so he has, on and off, ever since. The "fire planet" one is cool...the "ringed planet" one is cool...straight black hair is cool...you see before you one Watsuki Nobuhiro, falling to pieces....

Act 34—The State of Meiji Swordsmanship

Act 34
The State of Meiji Swordsmanship

OHH!
DON'T EVEN START!
HE HAD IT COMING.

ALL BEATEN UP, AS USUAL.
IS THERE ANY OTHER WAY?

SO YOU'RE HEADED OUT?
YUP. TODAY'S OUR OUTSIDE-TRAINING DAY.
WE'RE GOING TO THE MAEKAWA DOJO.
I KNOW! WHY DON'T *YOU* COME TODAY?
ORO?
THE MASTER, MAEKAWA-SENSEI, WANTS TO MEET YOU.
LAST TIME YOU WENT HOME RIGHT AWAY.
See Volume 1!

SORRY, NO CAN DO.
THERE'S LOGS TO CHOP, BATHS TO WARM, LAUNDRY...
OKAY, BUT THEN YOU'LL NEED TO SHOP, TOO.
I NEED MISO, SALT, RICE, AND SOY SAUCE. OH, AND VINEGAR.
PERHAPS THIS ONE CAN DO...
CLAP
NOW YOU'RE TALKING !!

THIS WILL BE SO MUCH FUN!!
OR NOT, THINKS THIS ONE.
WE READY? LET'S GO!!

ZZZOOOM

TP
VWIP VWIP
HF
HF
HF
THERE YOU ARE...
MASTER!!

......

IT TOOK A WHILE, BUT I THINK I GOT IT ALL.
DDD
UM, LET'S SEE...
FLIP FLIP
THERE ARE FOUR SWORD SCHOOLS IN THIS CITY.
ZP

THE *BUSIEST* ONE IS IN THE SOUTH OF THE CITY, DEVOTED TO CHŪETSU-RYŪ—MAEKAWA DOJO.
THE MASTER, MAEKAWA MIYAUCHI, HAS BEEN LIVING FOR NOTHING BUT SWORDS SINCE HE WAS A BOY.
PROBABLY THE BEST SWORDSMAN IN THE AREA.

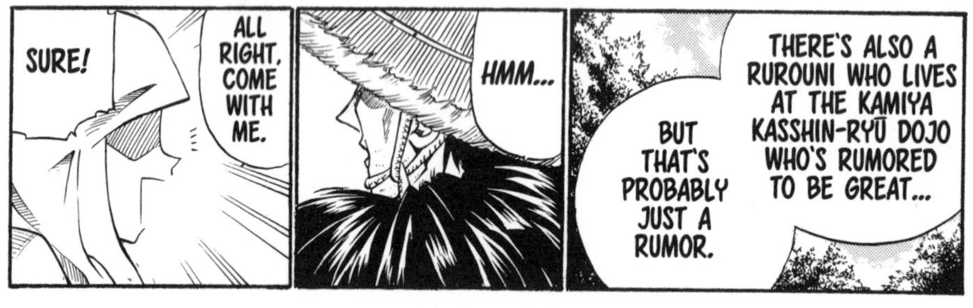
THERE'S ALSO A RUROUNI WHO LIVES AT THE KAMIYA KASSHIN-RYŪ DOJO WHO'S RUMORED TO BE GREAT...
BUT THAT'S PROBABLY JUST A RUMOR.
HMM...
ALL RIGHT, COME WITH ME.
SURE!

ZIP

中越流
前川道場
CHŪETSU-RYŪ MAEKAWA DOJO
HAI!!
BSSH
HEAD!!
PING
NOW. SWING PRACTICE, 50 STROKES.
BEGIN!!

KLATTA
KLAT
OH.
AH.
KON'NICHI WA!
YAAAAY!
KAORU-SAN!!
HIYA!

READ THIS WAY

HEY! HELLO!
WE'VE BEEN EXPECTING YOU. PLEASE, COME IN!
OH, DON'T MIND US. PLEASE CONTINUE WITH THE TRAINING.

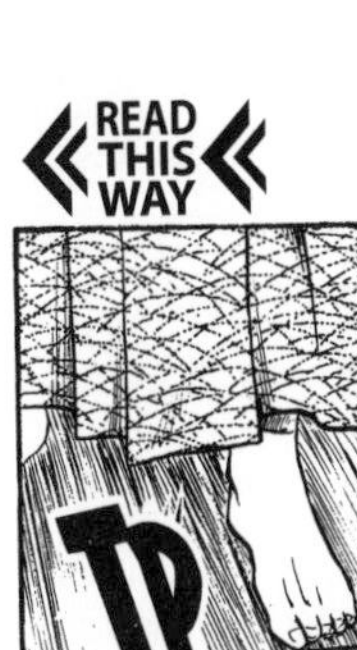

LISTEN TO KAORU-KUN. KEEP YOUR MINDS ON TRAINING.
TP

OH!

TP

MAEKAWA-SENSEI!

...SO. YOU MUST BE THE KENSHIN KAORU-KUN IS ALWAYS TALKING ABOUT.
TWIK

...RUROUNI, SUPPOSED TO BE POWERFUL...
YADA
YADA
...YEAH, I'VE SEEN HIM AROUND...

HIMURA KENSHIN...
...THE MAN THE SENSEI'S ALWAYS SAYING HE WANTS TO FIGHT.
!

......

WONDER WHO'D WIN...?
BLAH BLAH
YADA
YADA
THE SENSEI WOULD WIN, OBVIOUSLY. HE WAS IN THE "EDO TOP 20" WHEN HE WAS YOUNG.
WHAT...?
BLAH
MAEKAWA-SENSEI HAS NEVER SAID ANYTHING LIKE THAT TO ME...
BUT WHAT THEY SAY ABOUT THAT GUY...
BZZ BZZ

EITHER WAY, IT'S GONNA BE A MATCH WHERE NEITHER CAN HOLD BACK HIS STRENGTH.
THE LOSER WON'T GET OFF WITHOUT GETTING HURT.

HEH
HOH

HUH?

THANK YOU FOR COMING. WE LOOK FORWARD TO LEARNING FROM YOU.
BZZ BZZ
THIS ONE'S JUST HERE WITH KAORU-DONO, ACTUALLY...
YADA
BLAH
IS THAT SO? THEN PLEASE, MAKE YOURSELF COMFORT-ABLE.
I'LL HAVE SOME TEA PREPARED.
TP

SENSEI...
I'M SORRY I DIDN'T TELL YOU.
I DIDN'T THINK YOU WOULD BRING HIM IF I HAD.

IT'S THE SWORDS-MAN'S NATURE TO WISH TO FIGHT ANY STRONG OPPONENT.
DON'T TAKE IT AS AN INSULT.

BUT, SENSEI...
DON'T WORRY, KAORU-KUN. I'VE NO WISH TO FIGHT ANYMORE.
OH! LET ME DO...
NO. PLEASE.
I CAN SEE ALREADY THAT I'VE LOST.

↰ CUSHION

I GAVE HIM MY FIERCEST GLARE AND HIS EYES JUST LET IT FLOW AWAY.

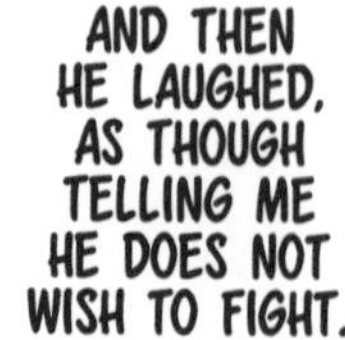

AND THEN HE LAUGHED, AS THOUGH TELLING ME HE DOES NOT WISH TO FIGHT.

THOSE EYES ARE...

...TRULY DEEP.

THERE'S SOMETHING IN HIS PAST HE DOESN'T SHARE WITH OTHERS.
TWIK
OF COURSE THERE IS.
HOW ELSE COULD HE HAVE SUCH EYES, AT HIS YOUNG AGE?

HE'S ACTUALLY 28.
.....
HE WHA-A-AT —!?
BUT THEN HE'D...!
?

HEY, HEY! DON'T BE SURPRISED JUST 'CAUSE HE COMES AT YOUR SIDE!!
RAM RAM RAM RAM
G-GOT IT.
RAM RAM
DON'T PULL YOUR BELLY BACK! AND, FIRST THING—WATCH YOUR OPPONENT'S EYES!!
RAM RAM RAM RAM RAM
RIGHT. NEXT!!
HMM...
WHAT DO YOU THINK OF OUR DOJO?
TP
...IT'S NICE.
YOU HAVE A LOT OF STUDENTS. IT'S LIVELY HERE.
USUALLY NOT EVEN A THIRD OF THEM SHOW.
BUT ON DAYS KAORU-KUN IS HERE...

THE FAMOUS "KENJUTSU PRINCESS" MAKES THEM *SWEAT.*
IT'S BECOME A SORT OF *ENTERTAINMENT* FOR THE YOUNG MEN.
THE NUMBER OF STUDENTS HAS SOARED SINCE KAORU-KUN STARTED COMING TO TRAIN HERE.

THERE MAY BE *TEN* OF THEM WHO ARE SERIOUS ABOUT SWORDS.
IT'S EMBARRASSING, BUT SUCH IS THE STATE OF THE DOJO THAT ONCE WAS CALLED "BEST IN EDO."

MORE EMBARRASSING STILL...
IS THAT I WOULD USE THE LEGACY OF *KAMIYA KOSHIJIRŌ* AS A TOOL TO ATTRACT STUDENTS.
YOU'RE TOO HARD ON YOURSELF, MAEKAWA-DONO.
THE KAMIYA DOJO, WHICH HAS SO FEW STUDENTS, BENEFITS FROM THIS AS WELL.
HELP AND BE HELPED.
HEH...
AGREED?
...HOH

STILL... WHAT IS TO BECOME OF KENJUTSU?
SWORD ARTS HAVE DECLINED SO QUICKLY SINCE THE DAYS OF MEIJI.
THE SEINAN WAR BROUGHT REVIVAL...
BUT SURELY IT CAN'T GO ON.
.....
HARD TO BELIEVE THAT ONCE...
...THERE CAME CHAL-LENGERS TO THE DOJO EACH DAY.
PWIK
?!

TMM
H-HEY. DON'T ENTER A DOJO WITH DIRTY FEET!
TAKE OFF YOUR SANDALS!!
TMMMMM
TMM
TMM
TMM
TMM
WHAT...? HEY!!

I BELIEVE YOU ARE THE FOUNDER OF CHŪETSU-RYŪ, MAEKAWA MIYAUCHI.
VSH
I REQUEST A MATCH WITH YOU.
I AM ISURUGI RAIJŪTA!!
SHA
WHO CARES FOR THE FUTURE OF KENJUTSU, YOU ASK...? I DO!
SHA

Act 35—"That Man" • Raijūta

Act 35
"That Man" • Raijūta

"RAIJŪTA," DID YOU SAY?

VERY WELL, I ACCEPT YOUR CHALLENGE.

HSP

BEST TWO-OUT-OF-THREE, IN THE POPULAR WAY.

AGREED?

TWIK

MAEKAWA-DONO...

I KNOW THIS IS NO AVERAGE MAN.
HE HAS THE SKILLS TO BACK UP THE STANCE.
THAT'S WHY I WANT TO FIGHT HIM.
HEH
.....
I MAY HAVE AGED, BUT I AM STILL THE SAME MAEKAWA MIYAUCHI WHO WAS CONSIDERED ONE OF THE "20 BEST."
I WILL NOT GO DOWN EASILY.
TP
...A SHINAI...
THIS ISN'T WORTH THE TIME.
WHAT ...?
RRK

READ THIS WAY

SHUT UP! WHO DO YOU THINK YOU ARE?!

BOOT

WHAT'RE YOU DOING, SQUIRT?!

YOU'RE THE SQUIRT.

YOU BOTH ARE.

ME, I'M THE FIRST STUDENT OF KAMIYA KASSHIN-RYŪ...

...MYŌJIN YAHIKO!

REMEMBER THAT NAME!

FIRST APPRENTICE OF RAIJŪTA-SENSEI...
...TSUKAYAMA YUTARŌ!
AND THAT *KICK'S* GONNA *COST* YOU!

QUIET.
THAT'S ENOUGH.
HA!
GG...
UN-FORTUNATELY, I DON'T *OWN* A SHINAI.
YOU'LL HAVE TO LOAN ME ONE.
PICK WHICHEVER YOU LIKE, BUT DON'T BLAME IT ON THE EQUIPMENT LATER.

...THIS WILL BE HARD FOR MAEKAWA-SENSEI TO WIN...
THERE'LL BE MANY BLOWS BUT, MOST LIKELY, THE LAST WILL BE FELT BY *HIM*...

If things go smoothly, the pace will start picking up in the series soon. It had been heading into a down-beat mode, which made me concerned about reader response. I know *RuroKen* ought to have an upbeat ending, so don't worry! It's been a year since the series started, so right now's the critical point. As of this volume, my own quibbles end—I'm going to start putting more "strength" into it, so please keep supporting me. I look forward to seeing you in the next volume!

伸宏和月

TO ASSURE FAIRNESS, THE JUDGE SHOULD REALLY BE FROM A DIFFERENT SCHOOL.
I'M KAMIYA KAORU. I'LL JUDGE.

ROUND ONE!

UUUWAH!!
WH...
TWIK TWIK
WHAT AN AURA!

WHEN YOU SUGGESTED A THREE-ROUND MATCH WITH A SHINAI...

...ALREADY, I KNEW YOU WERE "NOT WORTH THE TIME"!!

HSSS

!

PWIK

NO!

MAEKAWA-DONO, RUN—

NGH!

......!
SS
NNN!

I NEVER SAW HIM MAKE THE LEAP...

HE'S SO BIG... BUT SO FAST...

SO.

WAS THAT HIT *NULL?*

OH

VALID HEAD-HIT. ONE ROUND!

BLAH

BLAH

BLAH

WOW...

THE FIRST STRIKE WAS A MISS...BUT THAT *DOWN* SWING...

HEH. THAT WASN'T A MISS.

!

A STRIKE TO THE TOP OF THE HEAD SLIPS SOMETIMES BECAUSE OF THE SKULL.

SO IF YOU PLAN TO SWING *DOWN*, YOU SHOULD TARGET THE SHOULDER.

IN OLD-SCHOOL KENJUTSU, *EVERYBODY* KNOWS THAT.

IF THIS WAS FOR REAL, THAT OLD GUY...
...WOULD BE SAILING TO THE OTHER WORLD BY NOW.
SENSEI...
!

HIS SHOULDER'S BROKEN!
GET A DOC-TOR, QUI—
WAIT!
THIS MATCH ISN'T OVER YET.
WHAT?!
AS A SWORDS-MAN, I CANNOT RETREAT NOW.
GGG...
.....

BEGIN... THE NEXT ROUND!
.....
HIMURA-KUN.

ROUND TWO!!

YOU'RE ...

...NOT STOPPING YET?

HUF

HUF

HUF

THIS IS ABSURD! THIS WILL END WITH THE FIRST STRIKE!!

THWOK
CLEAN HIT!
MATCH OVER!
GRAB
!
GRP

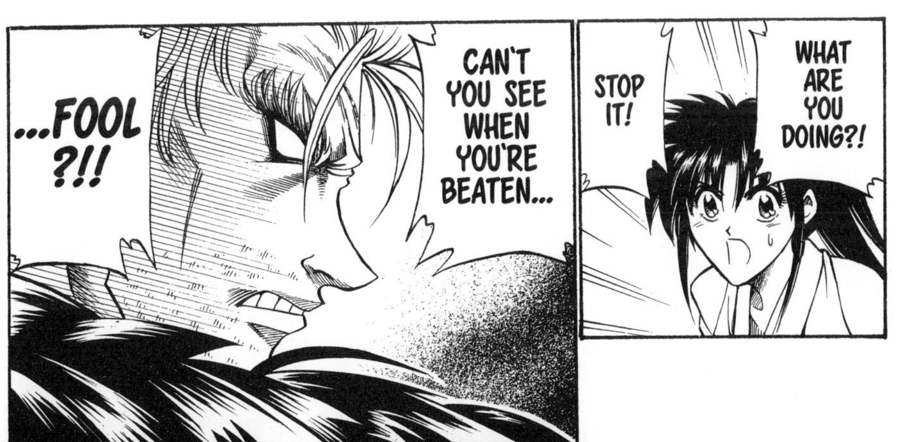

...THE MATCH IS OVER. YOU'VE WON.
SS
DO YOU MEAN TO KILL HIM?
.....
YES.

ONLY ONE LIFE IS GIVEN TO A MAN.
THERE IS NO SUCH THING AS A THREE-ROUND MATCH.
A MATCH IS *ONE* ROUND.
KILL, OR BE KILLED.

AFTER THE INVENTION OF THE SHINAI, KENJUTSU BECAME MORE *POPULAR.*
BUT IT LOST THE PURITY, THE *POWER* IT ONCE HAD.
THE ART OF THE SWORD BECAME A WEAK THING.

AND NOW IT ONLY GROWS WEAKER AND WEAKER!
THESE FOOLS WHO ARE HAPPY SWINGING AROUND SHINAI DO NOT *DESERVE* TO HOLD A SWORD!

EXCEPT...

...ONE OF *YOU!*

Rurouni
Kenshin

Act 36
Secret Sword

ARE YOU OF THIS DOJO?
NO... FOR NOW, THIS ONE IMPOSES UPON KAMIYA KASSHIN-RYŪ.

AH...SO YOU'RE THE *RUROUNI* WHO'S RUMORED TO BE SO STRONG.
WELL, THEN. I CHALLENGE *YOU* TO A MATCH.
TM
WITH *REAL* SWORDS.

THIS SWORD IS WIELDED...

NOT TO DISPLAY ONE'S OWN STRENGTH.

AS YOU CAN SEE...

KILLING IS WHAT THIS ONE AVOIDS.

YUTARŌ.
YES?
TAKE DOWN THE DOJO'S SIGN...
...AND BURN IT.

!!
I HAVE DEFEATED THE DOJO'S MASTER.
I AM FREE TO DO WHATEVER I *WANT* WITH THE SIGN.

IF YOU THINK DIFFERENTLY... COME AT ME.

ALL AT ONCE, IF YOU LIKE.

GNG

.....

IF WE'RE GOING TO DO THIS, LET'S DO IT IN THE STREET.

IT'LL BE A BETTER SHOW!

POM!

GRAB

HOLD IT RIGHT THERE...
...YOU LITTLE GOLDFISH TURD.
LET GO.
UNLESS YOU WANT TO DIE.

KAORU-SAN!
THIS ISN'T MY DOJO, BUT AS A DOJO MASTER, I CAN'T LET IT PASS.
EVEN IF I CAN'T BEAT YOU, I'LL GET IN A BLOW.
GLINT
.....
ARE YOU SURE?
I DON'T HOLD BACK... EVEN FOR WOMEN.
HSH

VERY WELL. THIS ONE WILL FIGHT.

!

BUT THE MATCH STAYS IN THE DOJO...

...AND, WE FIGHT WITH SHINAI.

...IF WE MUST, BUT A SINGLE ROUND ONLY.

YOU SURE ABOUT THIS?
YES.
ALTHOUGH THIS ONE IS UNFAMILIAR WITH A SHINAI...
BE CAREFUL.
THERE'S SOMETHING UP WITH THAT GUY.
HEH

WE'RE STARTING.
BUT THE JUDGE...
NO NEED.
TM
STAND READY!
TOOM

PIK

SSSHH

FINALLY WE GET TO SEE THE RUROUNI'S SKILLS!

YEAH ...

AS HE'S POUNDED INTO THE GROUND...

NN!!

HYOO
ZZZ ZUP
BYOO

......
DID YOU SEE THAT?
HUH?
SEE WHAT?
N-NOT REALLY, NO...
BUT...IT WAS *SOMETHIN'*.

**MUGYŌ*: POSITION WITH THE SWORD DOWN BY ONE HAND; *SEIGAN* (*CHŪDAN*): CUT TO MIDDLE-LEVEL.

WHY DON'T YOU STRIKE BACK?
ARE YOU TRYING TO INSULT ME?

NOT AT ALL.
AS SAID, THE SWORD IS NOT WIELDED TO SHOW THIS ONE'S STRENGTH.
...I SEE.
AND IF YOU FIGHT TO A DRAW, YOU CAN STOP MY TAKING THE SIGN.

IN THAT CASE...
TRY THIS!
SS
!
NN!

WHAT...
...IS THIS?

KEEEEEN

HMM...
WSH
TUP

WE'RE LEAVING.
TM
HUH?
OH...
OKAY!
DUNNO WHAT JUST WENT ON...
...BUT RAIJŪTA-SENSEI WAS ON TOP, ALL THE WAY.
I WOULDN'T BE SO SURE.
KENSHIN DIDN'T EVEN BRING *HALF* HIS STRENGTH.
YOU AND I WILL SETTLE THIS... SOMEDAY.

WHEN THAT DAY COMES, I'LL BEAT YOU BLUE, BLOODY, AND *RAW.*
FOOEY.

...SNOT-NOSED PUNK.
AND THAT KENSHIN'S GONNA GET HIS, TOO!
SO...HIS NAME IS KENSHIN...
SENSEI?

!
SENSEI IS SWEATING ...

NO ONE'S EVER DODGED MY *IZUNA*...MY "SECRET SWORD"...!
THAT MAN *KNOWS* THE ANCIENT ARTS...

HIS SKILL IS INCOMPARABLE!

WHOA

BZZ

YADA

BLAH

HE'S JUST WHAT I NEED FOR MY *SHINKO-RYŪ*!

WOW...
WHAT IS THIS?
YADA
YADA
BZZ
BLAH
IT'S LIKE THAT GUY WAS USING A SWORD...
BUT HOW CAN A SHINAI DO THAT?

NO, NOT LIKE A SWORD.
A SWORD COULD NEVER CUT SO SHARPLY.
IF HE USED THAT MOVE WITH A REAL SWORD...
...HE COULD CUT A *DIAMOND* IN HALF.

NO ORDINARY "SHOWBOAT FIGHTER" COULD DO THAT.

WHO *IS* THIS ISURUGI RAIJŪTA...?

Rurouni
Kenshin

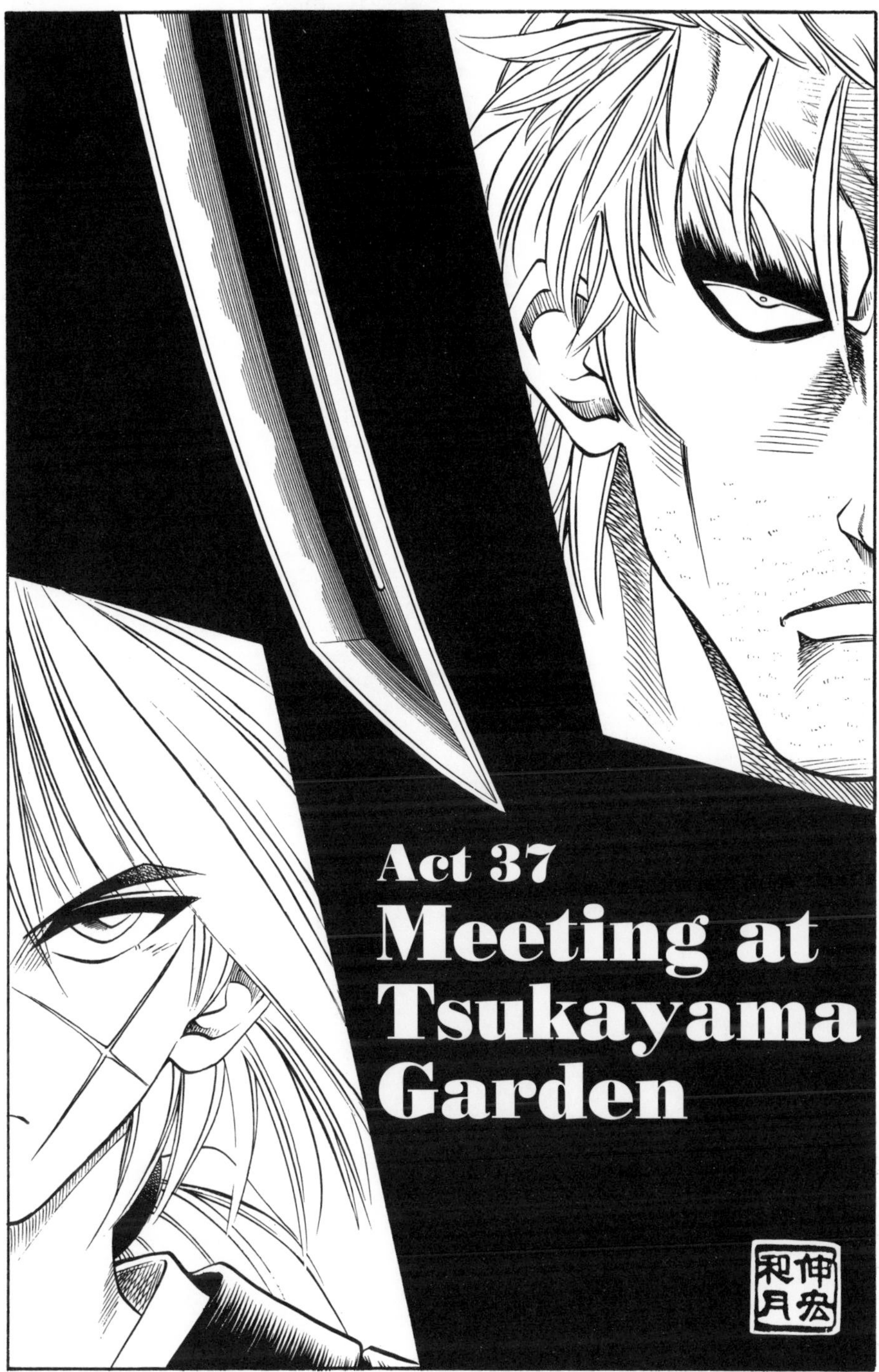
Act 37
Meeting at Tsukayama Garden
伸宏
和月

ISURUGI RAIJŪTA, HUH...?
INTERESTING GUY. SORRY I MISSED HIM.

I WOULDN'T SAY "INTERESTING"!!

VMMN NN

OOPS.

MAEKAWA DOJO IS CLOSING ITS DOORS BECAUSE OF HIM!!

HMMM.

SPOING

BUT ISN'T THAT HOW IT GOES?

BFF

VMN VMN VMN VMN

SPOING

!

READ
THIS
WAY

SURE, MAEKAWA GOT HIS ASS HANDED TO HIM...
...BUT IT WAS A LEGIT MATCH, RIGHT?

B—
BUT ...!

THERE'S NO ROOM FOR "SORTA" WHEN YOU RUN A DOJO. YOU CAN'T BLAME THE OTHER GUY FOR BEING "TOO STRONG."
RIGHT, KENSHIN?

TRUE ENOUGH, BUT...
THAT MAN WAS TOO STRONG. HE'S FAR PAST HAVING TO PROVE HIMSELF WITH DOJO CHALLENGES.

WHY DOES A MAN WHO DESPISES THE USE OF THE SHINAI, WHO USES SATSUJIN-KEN...
...GO AROUND CHALLENGING DOJO MASTERS?

EXCUSE ME...

!

MIGHT HIMURA KENSHIN-SAN...
...BE AVAILABLE NOW?

THIS ONE IS HIMURA.
OH, VERY GOOD.
HERE YOU ARE!
招待状
ZIP

READ
THIS
WAY

"INVITATION" ...?
YES.

!
石動雷十太
ISURUGI RAIJŪTA

WHAT'S THE MEANING OF THIS ...?
HE MEANS "LETTER OF CHALLENGE," RIGHT?
RIGHT?
ALAS, I AM ONLY THE BUTLER, SO...
IN ANY EVENT, I HAVE A CARRIAGE READY OUTSIDE.
DO COME.

THIS WAY, PLEASE.
I MUST SEE TO THE CARRIAGE... IF YOU GO THROUGH THE GARDEN, YOU WILL COME TO THE MAIN BUILDING.
......

READ THIS WAY

HEY, THIS "RAIJŪTA" GUY...
HE LOOK LIKE THIS?
SANOSUKE'S IMAGE
NOT EVEN!
HE'S SCRUFFY, LIKE...
KAORU'S IMAGE

YOU MUST BE HIMURA-SAN. THANK YOU FOR COMING.
!

IS THAT RAIJŪTA?
NO, IT IS NOT.

A PLEASURE TO MEET YOU. I OWN THIS HOUSE.
TSUKAYAMA YUZAEMON AT YOUR SERVICE.

TSUKAYAMA...
ARE YOU THE FATHER OF THAT LITTLE JERK...?

WHO'S A JERK, JERK?!
BOOT
!
ORO.

RAIJŪTA-SENSEI INVITED HIMURA ONLY!
WHY THE HECK ARE YOU—?!

YUTARŌ, STOP IT!
THESE ARE FRIENDS OF THE SENSEI'S GUEST. BE POLITE.
FUH!
I APOLOGIZE FOR MY SON'S RUDENESS.
BOW BOW
NO NEED.
I'LL GET YOU!

READ THIS WAY

THE SENSEI IS AT THE POND. I WILL LEAD YOU THERE.
YUTARŌ, YOU ENTERTAIN HIS FRIENDS.

WHAT-EVER. FOLLOW ME.
YOU CAN HAVE LEFTOVERS AND THE DREGS OF THE TEA.

MM-M... SUCH HOSPITALITY.
SORRY, BUT WE'LL HAVE TO DECLINE.
WOOSH

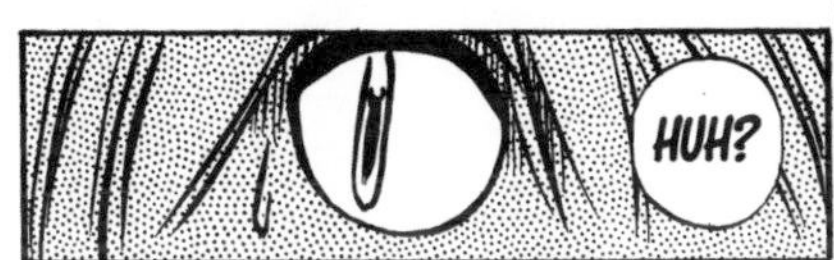
HUH?

...PRINCIPALLY, I AM AN EXPORTER OF SWORDS.

YOU MAY ALREADY KNOW THAT JAPANESE SWORDS FETCH A FINE PRICE IN EUROPE AS OBJECTS OF ART.

OF COURSE, PROSPERITY HAS ITS PRICE.
ABOUT THREE MONTHS AGO, A GANG OF BANDITS ATTACKED MY CARRIAGE.

RAIJŪTA-SENSEI HAPPENED TO BE PASSING, AND SAVED US.
SINCE THEN, I HAVE ASKED HIM TO BE MY GUEST AND TRAIN YUTARŌ IN SWORDS-MANSHIP.
A MAN MUST ALWAYS BE PREPARED FOR CONFLICT.
DON'T YOU AGREE?

...SENSEI.

PLEASE, TAKE YOUR TIME...

SHKA
SHK

HMM, SO *THAT'S* RAIJŪTA.
UM...ARE YOU SURE IT WAS ALL RIGHT TO DO THAT TO THE KID?
WHO CARES ABOUT HIM?
-THE KID-
......!
SANO-SUKE'S WRIST-WRAPS
YAHIKO'S SHINAI CORD
BUMP
THRASH

WHAT IS IT YOU WANT, RAIJŪTA?

HIMURA... WHAT DO YOU THINK OF TODAY'S SWORDSMAN-SHIP?

DON'T YOU BELIEVE IT'S WEAK?
STARVED IN SPIRIT?
IT'S GETTING WEAKER WITH EACH PASSING YEAR.

AND THE WEAK WILL ALWAYS BE CONQUERED.
THIS IS A LAW OF NATURE.

.....
AND SO...
ZAH!

READ THIS WAY

HIMURA, WILL YOU NOT JOIN US AND THE SHINKO-RYŪ...

...AND HELP *REVIVE* THE JAPANESE ART OF SWORDS?

ARE YOU ASKING THIS ONE TO BECOME YOUR STUDENT?
NO! TO BEGIN WITH, SHINKO-RYŪ HAS NO FORMS OR SKILLS.

YOU HAVE ONLY TO BE *STRONG.*
THAT'S ALL WE NEED OF OUR MEMBERS.

THEN IT'S NOT REALLY A SCHOOL. MORE LIKE A LEAGUE OF SWORDS-MEN...

YOU COULD CALL IT THAT. I'VE BEEN TO EVERY CORNER OF JAPAN, FIGHTING CHALLENGES AT DOJOS FOR YEARS.
I'VE FOUND PRECIOUS FEW SWORDSMEN WORTHY OF SHINKO-RYŪ.

OF THEM ALL, YOU'RE THE FIRST TO DODGE THE IZUNA.

EEEEEN
BLURR
SO THAT WAS...!

IF YOU JOIN MY COMRADES AND ME...

...WE COULD PUT AN END TO ALL 500 OF THE SCHOOLS OF "MODERN SWORDSMAN-SHIP."

AND WE WILL *NEVER* WEAKEN AGAIN... NOT EVER!

IN THE GLORY DAYS, EVEN BEFORE THE SENGOKU AGE OF WARLORDS, SWORDSMEN WERE SO POWERFUL THAT WE WERE FEARED AS MAGICIANS—"USERS OF THE WHIRLWIND"!

WE OF SHINKO-RYŪ WILL BE SUCH MAGICIANS AGAIN—AND BRING THE WHIRLWIND *BACK* TO JAPAN!!!

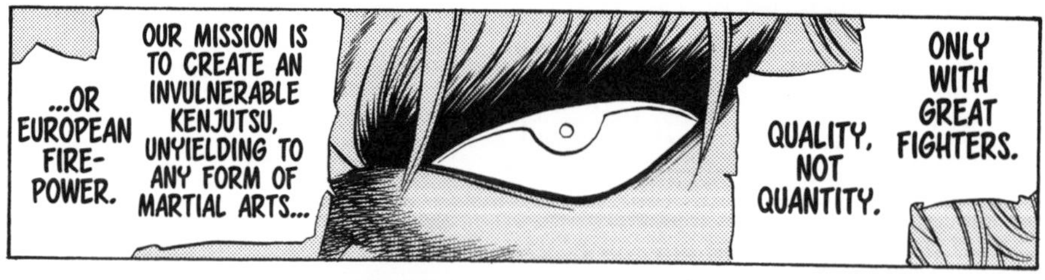

ONLY WITH GREAT FIGHTERS.
QUALITY, NOT QUANTITY.
OUR MISSION IS TO CREATE AN INVULNERABLE KENJUTSU, UNYIELDING TO ANY FORM OF MARTIAL ARTS...
...OR EUROPEAN FIRE-POWER.

WHAT IS HE *THINKING?*
IT'S EXTREME, ALL RIGHT... BUT HE HAS A POINT...
IF SWORDFIGHTING IS PASSED ON ONLY TO THE TALENTED...
...AS IS KABUKI, IT REALLY *COULD* STAY PURE.

LEND YOUR STRENGTH TO ME...

HIMURA.

ANCIENT KENJUTSU IS A "SATSUJIN-KEN"... MEANT FOR REAL WAR.

ARE YOU AWARE OF THAT?

OF COURSE.

BUT KENJUTSU IS THE ART OF *KILLING* TO BEGIN WITH!

THIS "SHINAI KENJUTSU" IS A SHAM.

IF YOU TRULY THINK SO...THEN THIS ONE AND YOU WILL *NEVER* AGREE.

!

HSS

HIMURA.
DO YOU EVEN *CARE* IF JAPANESE KENJUTSU DIES?
.....
.....
OF COURSE.
AS A SWORDSMAN...
THE FUTURE OF SWORDS MUST BE CONSIDERED.
BUT IF THE FUTURE MEANS A RETURN TO WANTON *KILLING*...
...THIS ONE WANTS NO PART OF IT.

READ THIS WAY

THERE'S NO DISPUTING KENJUTSU IS A COMBAT ART. GO START SHINKO-RYŪ IF YOU THINK YOU MUST.
BUT IF YOU'RE GOING TO CRUSH ANYONE WHO DOESN'T SEE IT YOUR WAY...
YOU MUST ALSO EXPECT THIS ONE TO *STOP* YOU.

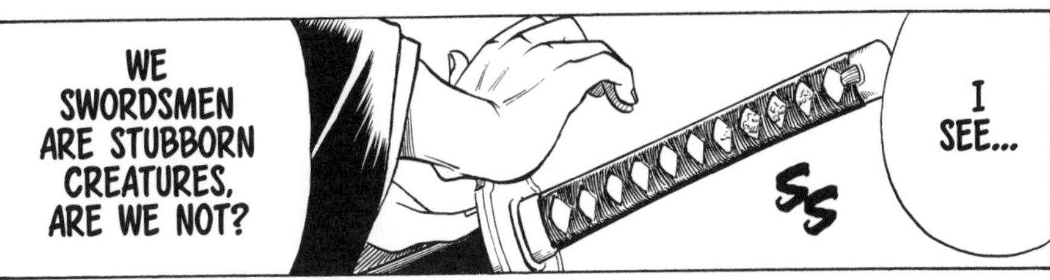
I SEE...
SS
WE SWORDSMEN ARE STUBBORN CREATURES, ARE WE NOT?

WE CAN ONLY COMMUNICATE ...
...THROUGH OUR *BLADES.*
KLINT

Rurouni
Kenshin

Act 38
Yutarō's Skill

.....

THEY AREN'T MOVING ...
BOTH WAITING FOR THE OTHER TO MOVE FIRST.
NEITHER'S THE KIND OF OPPONENT YOU JUST *CHARGE* OUTRIGHT...

HYOOOOO

READ THIS WAY
UWOO
HH
NN!!!

PWEE

READ THIS WAY

OHH!!

SKK

SO *THIS* IS A MATCH BETWEEN TWO GREAT SWORDS-MEN!

IT *IS* DRAMATIC, ISN'T IT?!

OH...DON'T MIND ME. KEEP GOING.
TSK
I'LL JUST LEAVE THE TEA HERE.

THE MOMENT'S BEEN LOST. WE'LL POSTPONE THIS.
BUT DON'T FORGET.

YOU *WILL* LEND ME YOUR STRENGTH, OR YOU *WILL* DIE BY MY HAND.
THOSE ARE THE ONLY TWO PATHS.

NEITHER IS ACCEPTED.
FEH...
SHK
SHK
WELL, GUESS IT'S OVER FOR NOW...
FEEL LIKE I'M FORGETTING SOMETHING ...
UMM
YEAH, BUT WHAT ...?
OH!

READ THIS WAY

NONE OF YOU, NOT A ONE...
...WILL I *EVER* FORGIVE!!
GASP

ALL RIGHT, ALL RIGHT.
DON'T GET YOUR SHORT-PANTS IN A BUNCH.
PAT PAT
DON'T YOU "PAT" ME!!
NO REMORSE

THE DAY WILL COME WHEN YOU *RUST* ON MY SWORD!!
...YOU TIED HIM TO A TREE?
SANOSUKE, NOT ME.
YOU'RE ALL NOISE!!
WHAT?!!
IF YOU'VE GOT ENOUGH ENERGY TO SQUEAL LIKE A LITTLE BABY...
YOU'VE GOT ENOUGH TO FACE *ME*, ALONE!

BUT...
WITH A SHINAI!
.....
YOU...
...YOU PUNK!!
AND THEN...
THE NEXT DAY...
GLEAM
DOOM

READ THIS WAY

I CAME LIKE YOU SAID, SHORTY!

UMM... DO YOU REALIZE WHAT TIME IT IS?

WE DIDN'T SET A TIME!!

NOW FIGHT ME!!

I'M ENDING THIS! YOU BETTER BE READY!

HEH!

HEY KAORU, BE THE JUDGE!

NNN~~~~
Low Blood Pressure
WOBBLE
WOBBLE
ROUND ONE. GO.

FIRST ROUND!!

I'LL GET YOU LATER!

LET'S GO!!

HYAH!

!

OH?

ORO?

READ THIS WAY

HEY, AREN'T YOU HOLDING THE SHINAI WRONG?
GULP
!!!
YOU DON'T NORMALLY PUT YOUR HANDS TOGETHER. YOU HOLD THE END OF IT, LIKE *THIS*...

LOOK, I'VE ONLY BEEN TRAINED FOR *REAL* SWORDS!
SO WHAT IF I DON'T KNOW HOW TO HOLD A SHINAI?!

REAL SWORDS AND SHINAI ARE HELD THE SAME WAY...
.....
COULD IT BE...THAT YOU WERE JUST BLUFFING ALL THIS TIME...
...AND DON'T EVEN *KNOW* HOW TO FIGHT?!

RRRG
BULL'S-EYE

OHO! SO THAT'S WHY YOU CAME SO EARLY! TO CATCH ME WHILE I WAS SLEEPY!

......

BRR
BRR
BRR

WHAT A WASTE OF TIME.

RAIJŪTA DOESN'T TEACH YOU?

門下生
明神弥彦

ZP

IT'S NOT HIS FAULT.

HE'S BUSY WITH HIS SHINKO-RYŪ.

HE SAYS JAPANESE SWORDSMANSHIP NEEDS SHINKO-RYŪ.

I CAN'T BE SELFISH AND GET IN THE WAY.

READ
THIS
WAY

CAN'T BE HELPED. OKAY...
SINCE YOU CAME ALL THIS WAY, I'LL TEACH YOU.
神谷活心流
HUH?

FIRST: THE WAY TO HOLD A SHINAI.
HOOK YOUR LEFT PINKY ON THE END OF THE SHINAI LIKE THIS...
SHF

WHY'RE YOU BLUSHING, YOU...
YOU PERVERT ?!
SH-SHADDUP !!
YAHIKO, STOP TEASING HIM!
FOOEY!

HEAD!
HEAD!
HEAD!
HEAD!
HEAD!
HEAD!
神谷薫
門下生
明神弥彦
VNG
HEAD
!!!
THAT'S IT. KEEP IT UP!
YUTARŌ, YOU'RE GOOD!
CLAP
CLAP
!
REALLY
?!
REALLY. YOU HAVE PROMISE!
YEAH!
GLOOM

READ THIS WAY

TIME FOR A REST.

NONE OF YOU HAVE EATEN SINCE MORNING SO, HERE'S *ONIGIRI.*

HERE, YAHIKO.

MG.

GLOOM

STUPID KAORU.

TAKING THAT GUY'S SIDE.

GLP GLP

HERE, YUTARŌ.
DON'T WANT IT.

YOU ARE MY SENSEI'S ENEMY.
CAN'T TAKE STUFF FROM THE ENEMY.

DON'T BE STUBBORN. THE SENGOKU WARLORD UESUGI KENSHIN WAS SAID TO HAVE SENT SALT TO ENEMY GENERALS.

KENSHIN SPEAKS OF KENSHIN.

!
PLUS, THIS SHOULD BE SAFER THAN THE ONES KAORU-DONO MADE.
.....

...AN-N-NYWAY...
HEY, NOT SO CLOSE, HUH?!

HOW IS IT?
IS KENJUTSU WITH SHINAI FUN?

READ THIS WAY

...WHAT, SINCE IT'S JUST PLAY?
PLAY IS SUPPOSED TO BE *FUN*, RIGHT?

BUT THIS IS IT FOR ME. PLAYING...
WON'T GET ME STRONGER.
ORO?

I'M GOING TO BE AN INVINCIBLE SWORDSMAN LIKE THE SENSEI, AND SHOW MY FATHER!
YOU'RE GOING TO "SHOW" HIM...?
YEAH.
HE THREW AWAY HIS PRIDE AS A SAMURAI AND BECAME A MERCHANT. HE BOWS AND GRINS AND PRETENDS TO LAUGH TO CURRY FAVOR. HE SELLS SWORDS, THE SOUL OF THE SAMURAI, TO FOREIGN COUNTRIES.
I'M GOING TO SHOW HIM HOW A TRUE SAMURAI *LIVES* BY HIS SWORD!

IS THAT RIGHT...?
SO THE BOY HAS PRIDE LIKE YAHIKO'S, BUT A DIFFERENT REASON TO FIGHT.

BUT IF YOU DON'T GET TAUGHT, YOU'LL NEVER BE STRONGER.
UGH ...!

YUTARŌ, IF YOU'RE UP TO IT...
...WHY NOT JOIN THIS DOJO?
!

GASP
WHAT?!

PUT ASIDE YOUR DESIRE TO "SHOW" YOUR FATHER...
JOIN THE TRAINING SESSIONS WITH A PURE WILL TO LEARN KENJUTSU.

PLUS, IF YOU AND YAHIKO COMPETE WITH EACH OTHER...
YOU'LL IMPROVE FASTER!
...
KAMIYA KASSHIN-RYŪ.
THIS MUST BE IT.
神谷活心流
剣術道場
THE OPPONENT IS A MAN THE SENSEI HAS ACKNOWLEDGED.
DO NOT LET YOUR GUARDS DOWN!

Act 39
Clash

和月伸宏

ME...
JOIN KAMIYA KASSHIN-RYŪ?
WHY NOT?
THOUGH IT'S UP TO YOU, YUTARŌ-KUN.
MM... THE IDEA HAS ITS MERITS.
YEAH... LIKE NONE!!
BOO BOO
WHO NEEDS THAT SECOND-RATE PUNK?!

WHAT ARE YOU AND KENSHIN *THINKING?!*

HE'S RAIJŪTA'S APPRENTICE !!

ARE YOU...
NN?

...AFRAID THAT, IF I TRAIN, I'LL BECOME STRONGER THAN YOU?
GRIN
SNAP

IDIOT! YOU'LL NEVER GET ANY STRONGER, NO MATTER WHAT YOU DO!
WHAT DID YOU SAY, SHORTY?!
DMM DMM
TWIK
SSSSS
EVERYONE— TO THE WALL!

KIEEE!!
DDDDD
ZUD
HSH
?!
VEE

WHAT?!

SHIM
MMM

EXCUSE US. WE ARE...
THE HAT IS HINT ENOUGH.
RAIJŪTA'S COMRADES, FROM SHINKO-RYŪ?

YES. THEN THE CHAT WILL BE SHORT. I WILL SIMPLY ASK YOU.
SS
WILL YOU BECOME OUR COMRADE?
PLEASE CONSIDER YOUR CHOICES.

WHETHER YOU'RE HERE TO ARGUE OR TO THREATEN...
...STILL YOU'VE NO HOPE OF CHANGING THE DECISION.

THEN DEATH AWAITS YOU!!
DD
KENSHIN!!
TO THREATEN, THEN.
I'LL HAVE YOUR HEAD!!
!
JAB!

KEEEN

NNNN

GWNN

WHA—

KREET KREET KREET

OOOOOOM

UH...

TH... THIS MAN ...

NO WONDER THE SENSEI SPEAKS HIGHLY OF YOU.
BUT CAN YOU TAKE THE THREE OF US, AT THAT PACE?
YOU MEAN... *TWO* OF YOU.
URRAH
!

DOOOOM
!

DM
W-WHEN WE STRUCK HIM TWO-ON-ONE...
HE KNOCKED OUT A THIRD... IN MID-AIR!!

......

FINE.
I WILL GO.
SSS
CHK

KEEEN
!
RRR RRR
RRR
HE ATTACKED FASTER THAN KENSHIN—THERE'S NO ROOM FOR A COUNTER-ATTACK!
TING
THIS GUY...
HE'S GOOD!!!
HOOH
NUUUU!!

!!
HYOH!

I... SEE.
YOU ARE TOO STRONG.
I SEE WHY THE SENSEI WISHED TO DESTROY YOU...
...IF YOU WOULD NOT... JOIN US.
ZANNG
AIEEE!
!
VM

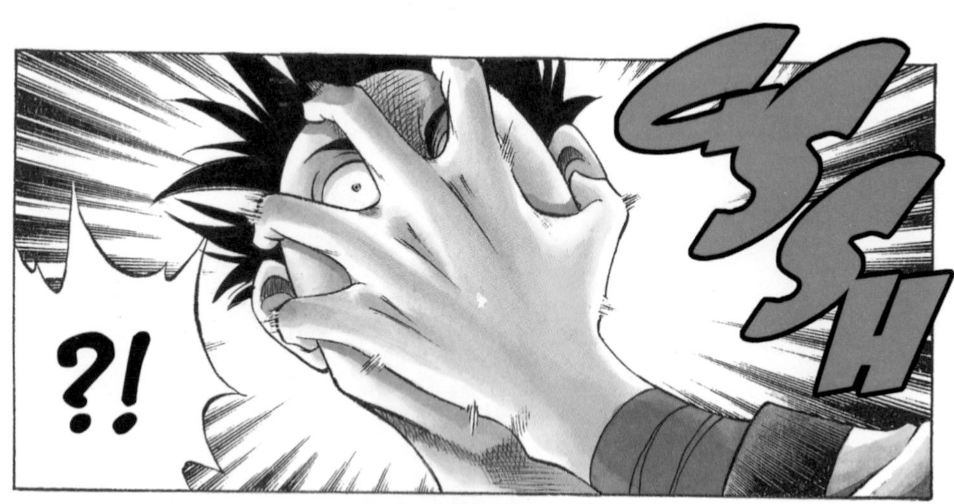

RUNNING AWAY ALONE, LEAVING YOUR COMRADES BEHIND.

GNG GNG

THAT DON'T IMPRESS ME MUCH.

G... GGGG...

LET HIM GO, SANO. THERE'S NO POINT...

...IN CHASING ONE WHO'S LOST THE WILL TO FIGHT.

GO HOME AND TELL RAIJŪTA...

...NO TRICKS. NO ALLIES. JUST TO COME BY HIMSELF.

OR, TO STOP MAKING THIS ONE FIGHT...
...BATTLES NOT WANTED.

FOO. WHY AM I ALWAYS GONE...
WHEN YOU HAVE THE *FUN* FIGHTS?
悪
.....
PERHAPS TO *YOU* THEY ARE FUN.

KENSHIN HASN'T EVEN SHOWN...
...*HALF* HIS REAL STRENGTH.

THIS GUY REALLY IS...
...POWERFUL !!

Rurouni Kenshin

VOLUME 6: No Worries

伸宏
和月

Act 40
The Ideal Man
伸宏
和月

IT'S BEEN TEN DAYS SINCE SHINKO-RYŪ ATTACKED...
BUT STILL NO SIGN OF RAIJŪTA.
DID THEY GET SCARED BECAUSE YOU BEAT 'EM SO EASILY?
IT WASN'T ALL THAT EASY.
THAT MAN WITH THE DOUBLE BLADES, HE WAS QUITE A SWORDSMAN.

SOMEHOW I DON'T QUITE BUY THAT...
DON'T YOU?
KATTA
WHO YOU CALLIN' A MINIATURE MONKEY, YOU CAT-EYED FREAK?!
UH-OH.
ORO.

WHY ARE YOU HERE TRAINING EVERY DAY WHEN YOU AREN'T EVEN A STUDENT?!

I THOUGHT YOU WERE TOO *GOOD* FOR SHINAI SWORD FIGHTING!!

SHINAI ARE FOR *KIDS!!*

BESIDES, I ONLY CAME TO GATHER INFO ON THE RAIJŪTA-SENSEI AND HIMURA KENSHIN BATTLE.

WHAT'S TO GATHER? ALL HE DOES ALL DAY ARE *CHORES.*
I *KNOW!*
IS HE A SWORDSMAN OR A MAID??

YOU DON'T LIKE IT, *LEAVE!!*
YOWW!
AND WHY SHOULD I LISTEN TO YOU?!
YOWW!
THE MAIN EVENT'S NOT HERE, BUT THE *SIDESHOW* IS.
EVERY DAY FOR THE PAST TEN DAYS...

RRG! THESE KIDS!
ALL RIGHT!! ENOUGH!!

BOTH OF YOU, START PRACTICING!
CLAP
CLAP
ACK!
GRG!
HEY, YAHIKO.
HUH?
YUTARŌ HAS TO PRACTICE HIS LUNGING.
LET HIM PRACTICE ON YOU.

WHY ME?! FORGET IT!!
BECAUSE THERE'S TOO MUCH *HEIGHT DIFFERENCE* WITH ME.

SO QUIT GRUMBLING.

PUT ON A MASK... THAT'S AN ORDER!

PFUI!

流心活谷神

ZAH!

READ THIS WAY

SO LUNGE, ALREADY.
I'M GONNA BE TAKING YOUR LAME ATTACKS, SO YOU BETTER THANK ME FOR...
SS
SS
!

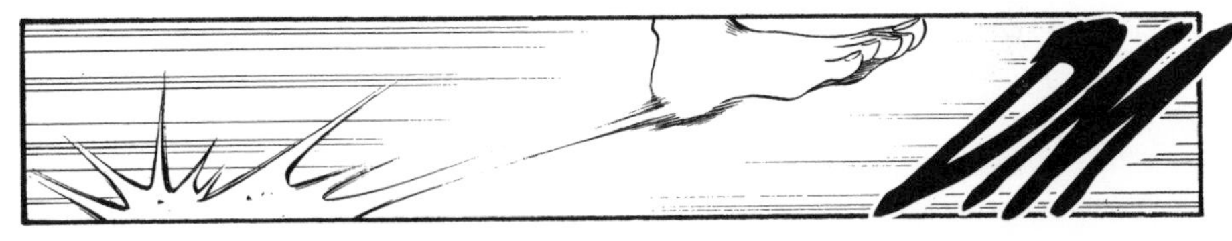
DM

HEAD!
BAM!
HO!

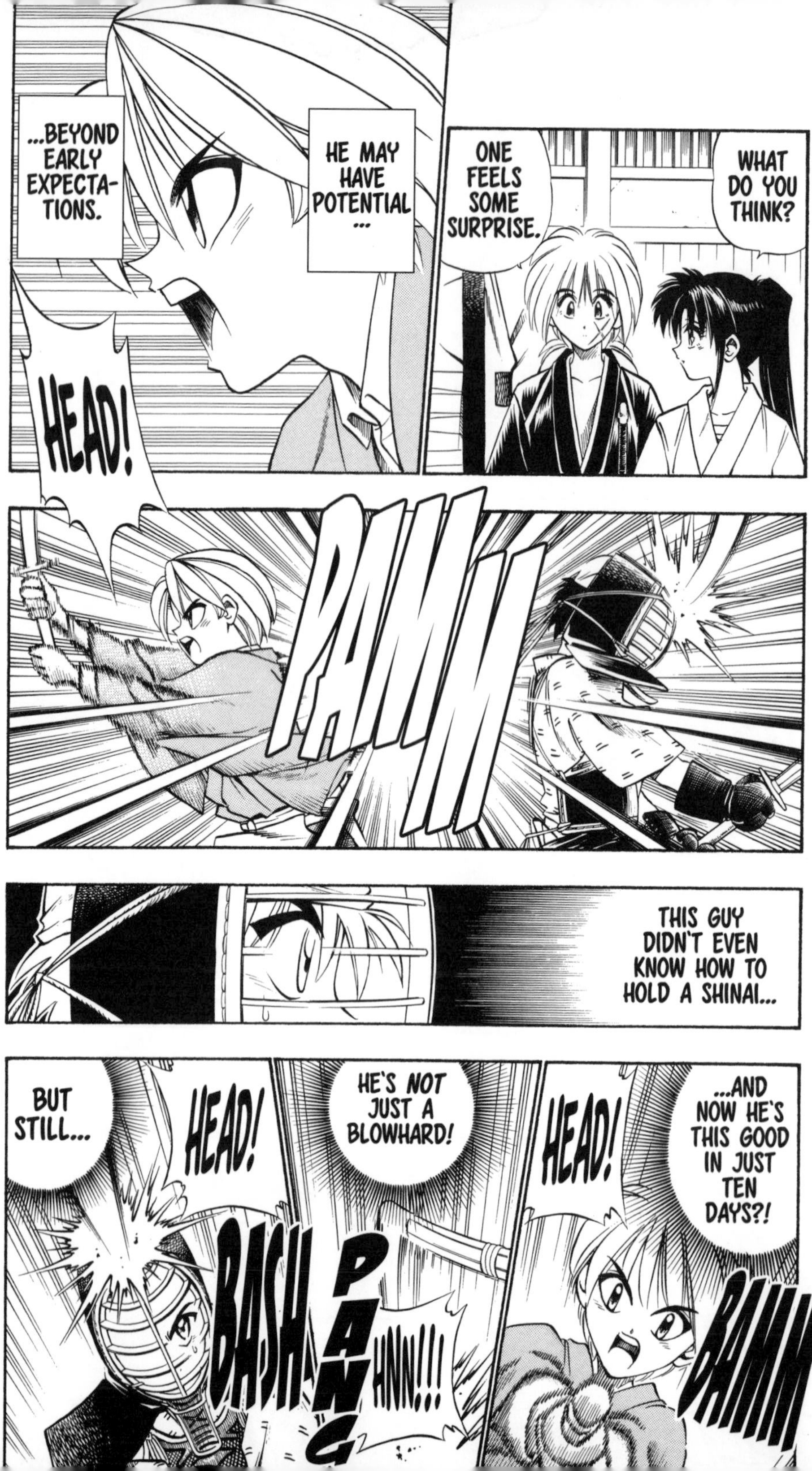

WHAT DO YOU THINK?
ONE FEELS SOME SURPRISE.
HE MAY HAVE POTENTIAL...
...BEYOND EARLY EXPECTATIONS.
HEAD!
PAMM

THIS GUY DIDN'T EVEN KNOW HOW TO HOLD A SHINAI...

...AND NOW HE'S THIS GOOD IN JUST TEN DAYS?!
HEAD!
HE'S *NOT* JUST A BLOWHARD!
PANG
BUT STILL...
HEAD!
BASHAHNN!!!

I'M GETTING SICK OF YOU HITTING ME!!
GONG
GONG
BRING IT!!
GONG
STOP IT!! STOP IT!!
GONG
ORO-RO.

Long time no see. Watsuki here. Below are the results of a popularity contest held between the staff (five of them...and, no, I wasn't included).

1st: Takani Megumi (26 points)
2nd: Shinomori Aoshi (16 points)
3rd: Nagaoka Mikio (10 points)
3rd: Myōjin Yahiko (10 points)
3rd: Sanjō Tsubame (10 points)
3rd: Sagara Sōzō (10 points)
7th: Udō Jin-e (9 points)
8th: Sagara Sanosuke (8 points)
9th: Beshimi (7 points)
10th: Isurugi Raijūta (5 points)
10th: Zanza (5 points)
12th: Kamiya Kaoru (4 points)

Pretty funny, in that it's totally different from the popularity poll conducted in the magazine! Megumi got a vote from every staffer, so she's first. Aoshi got his votes because the staff knows what's coming in the future, and Nagaoka, he's just plain popular 'round these parts. Sano and Zanza got separate votes because that's how the staff sees them and, interestingly, Kenshin got NO votes at all! Whoa, whoa—what's up with THAT?!

Watsuki

酒処
牛鍋
赤べこ
YADA
YADA
YADA
PHEW!
NOTHING LIKE A MEAL AFTER GOOD EXERCISE!
HEY, YOU! I WANT SECONDS!
SNAP
WE GOT NO FOOD TO WASTE ON YOU!!
THAT'S HOW YOU TALK TO A CUSTOMER ?!
YOU'RE NOT STOPPING THEM?
I GIVE UP.
UMM...

OH, TSUBAME-CHAN!
THANK YOU FOR THE OTHER DAY.
Akabeko's New Uniform
HAS NAGAOKA BOTHERED YOU SINCE?
NO... THANKS TO YOU.
ANYTHING ELSE HAPPENS, YOU JUST LET US KNOW.
UM... IS THAT A FRIEND OF YAHIKO-KUN?
UH... SOMETHING LIKE THAT.
THEY SURE SEEM... FRIENDLY.
PWIK
WE'RE FIGHTING, HERE!
HOW IS THAT "FRIENDLY"?!
HOW BLIND CAN YOU BE?!
GYAH
S... SORRY...!

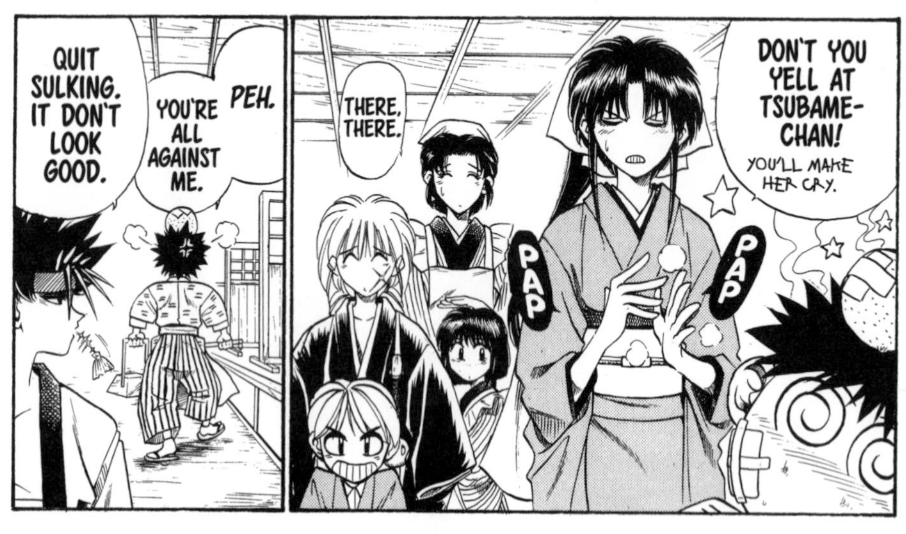

DON'T YOU YELL AT TSUBAME-CHAN!
YOU'LL MAKE HER CRY.
PAP
PAP
THERE, THERE.
PEH.
YOU'RE ALL AGAINST ME.
QUIT SULKING. IT DON'T LOOK GOOD.

OH, BY THE WAY, YUTARŌ...
WE WERE TALKING...
CHOMP
CHOMP
TALKING? 'BOUT WHAT?
ABOUT HAVING YOU JOIN THE KAMIYA DOJO.
PING

HOW ABOUT IT? I THINK YOU'LL DO WELL.

YOU AND YAHIKO CAN BE THE FIRST GRADUATES OF THE NEW KAMIYA KASSHIN-RYŪ.

READ THIS WAY

......

TAK

赤べこ

!

I'M SORRY.

KAORU-SAN, YOU'RE A GREAT TEACHER, AND I'M PLEASED THAT YOU SEE SO MUCH IN ME.
AND I CAN SEE THAT HIMURA KENSHIN IS A TRULY GREAT SWORDSMAN.

I'VE ENJOYED TRAINING AT THE KAMIYA DOJO.
I SCORNED SHINAI SWORDSMANSHIP, BUT I'VE LEARNED NOW HOW MUCH FUN IT IS.
DON'T CARE MUCH FOR "BIRD-HEAD," HERE...
LIKE I CARE WHAT YOU THINK.

EVEN SO, I STILL...
WANT TO MASTER THE BLADE...
...UNDER RAIJŪTA-SENSEI.

....

READ THIS WAY
I FIRST MET THE MASTER ON A NIGHT LIKE THIS.
WE WERE FOLLOWING A FOREST PATH BACK TO THE MANSION...
...WHEN OUR CARRIAGE WAS ATTACKED BY BANDITS.
GWAH!!

AAA!!
HOO HOO HOO...
HEH HEH HEH...
GO AHEAD AND CALL FOR HELP, TSUKAYAMA-SAN.
NOBODY WILL HEAR YOU SO FAR FROM THE CITY.
YOU ...!!
ZP

I'LL GIVE YOU WHATEVER YOU WANT.
JUST, PLEASE... DON'T HURT US.
FATHER!!
HEH. LOOK AT HIM.
DID YOU EXCHANGE YOUR PRIDE FOR MONEY, ALONG WITH YOUR SWORD?
YOU, TOO, BOY. GROVEL AND BEG FOR YOUR LIFE.
NEVER!!
I'M A SAMURAI OF TOKYO... TSUKAYAMA YUTARŌ!

HEH.
YAUGH!!
YUTARŌ!!
QUIT ACTING TOUGH, KID.
TUG
YOU SHOULD LEARN FROM YOUR FATHER. BEG LIKE HIM.
RIGHT, TSUKAYAMA-SAN?
GOK
PLEASE... SPARE OUR LIVES!
HYAA-HAHA!!
FATHER...

HUH?
!!

JUST—
—ONE STRIKE !!
THAT ONE STRIKE SETTLED IT!
THE ROBBERS SCATTERED LIKE BABY SPIDERS.
IN THAT MOMENT, I BELIEVED HE WAS INVINCIBLE.

THE SENSEI IS A MAN OF FEW WORDS, SO PEOPLE MISUNDERSTAND HIM.
RAIJŪTA ACTUALLY *HELPING* PEOPLE?
NOW I *KNOW* YOU'RE LYING.
SHUT UP, BIRD-HEAD!!

THAT WAS THE FIRST AND LAST TIME I SAW HIM WITH A REAL SWORD...
BUT I'VE KNOWN EVER SINCE THAT I WANTED TO HAVE HIS POWER...POWER ENOUGH TO DEFEAT *ANYTHING.*

IF I CAN BE STRONG LIKE HIM...
I'LL NEVER HAVE TO LIVE IN DISGRACE, LIKE MY FATHER.
HIMURA KENSHIN, YOU AND MY SENSEI WILL FIGHT SOMEDAY, WON'T YOU?
WHEN THAT TIME COMES, FACE HIM FAIR AND SQUARE.
THAT IS HOW TWO INVINCIBLE MEN *SHOULD*—

SENSEI ?!!
!!
HOH HOH

Rurouni Kenshin

Act 41–The Second Secret Sword
!

Act 41
The Second Secret Sword
THIS CAN'T BE...
...MY MASTER ??
伸宏
和月

ZZZZ
ZZZZ

USING *IZUNA* WITH A *REAL* SWORD!
SO HE COMES TO KILL— NO MATTER *HOW* HE HAS TO DO IT!

TSK

SURPRISE ATTACKS FROM BEHIND, IN THE DARK, EH?
HEH
SEEMS WE'RE FINALLY SEEING YOUR *TRUE* NATURE.

NO! THAT WAS JUST A GREETING!

HE NEVER *MEANT* FOR THAT STRIKE TO LAND!

RIGHT, SENSEI?!

NNN!!!

NRRAAAHH!!
!
!!

!

TP

JUST LIKE MY ZANBATŌ.

NO MATTER HOW POWERFUL THE BLOW, IT'S NOTHING UNLESS IT HITS.

NNN!

BLINDING ...?

SENSEI !!

BF

NNK
KEEEN
NOT GOOD ENOUGH.
HYOO
RYŪTSUISEN!!
NGH!

READ THIS WAY

......

SHK

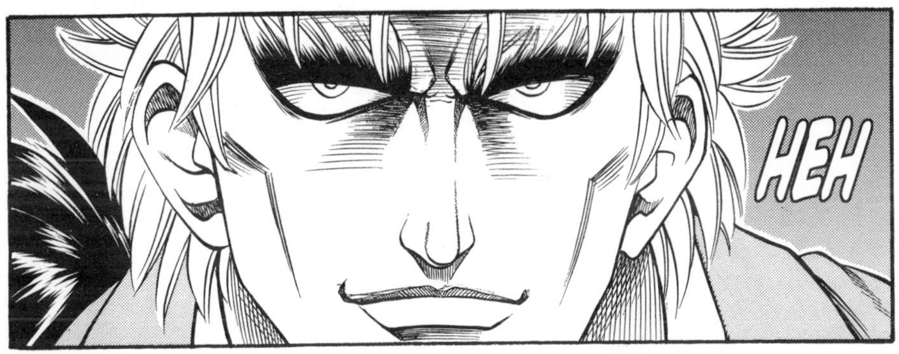

THIS LAST IZUNA IS LEFT TO ME...
AND YOU LEAVE ME NO CHOICE!!
SECRET SWORD...
TOBI IZUNA!!

ZSCH
KLEEN
WHAT—?!
?

DOOM
!!!!

READ THIS WAY

NO!!
YUTARŌ !!
FFP
BLUP
WE HAVE TO STOP THE BLEEDING, GET HIM TO A DOCTOR...
!

LEAVE HIM BE.

I MISSED HIS VITALS. HE'LL LIVE.

WHAT?!

YOU INJURED YOUR OWN APPRENTICE! DON'T YOU SEE THAT?!

YOU ARE THE ONE WHO DOES NOT SEE.

TM

TM

YOU CAN'T REALLY THINK I'D TAKE A *FOOL* LIKE *THAT* UNDER MY WING...?

WHAT... DID YOU...?

READ THIS WAY

YOU KNOW HOW LITTLE MONEY IS MADE FROM SWORDSMANSHIP IN THIS MODERN WORLD.
STILL, A LARGE SUM IS NEEDED TO BUILD SHINKO-RYŪ.
A MAN IN MY POSITION NEEDS A PATRON.

YET MY PATRON HAS *THIS* WHELP...
SO, YES, I LET THE FOOL CALL ME "SENSEI."

IT'S A SHAME TO LOSE SUCH A RICH PATRON, BUT I CAN ALWAYS FIND ANOTHER. AND I CAN ALWAYS HIRE MORE GOONS...
!!

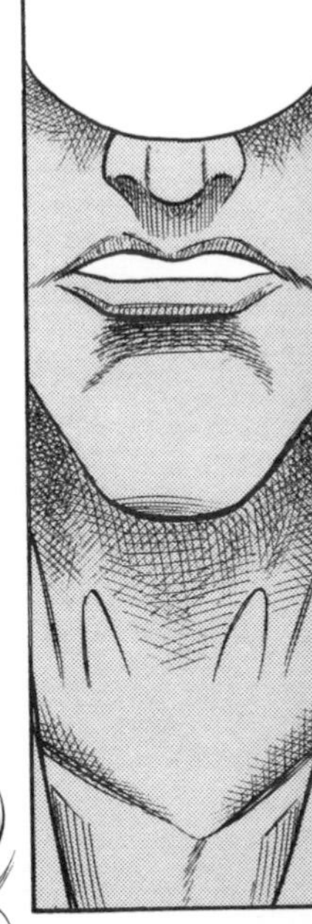

...TO *FAKE* ANOTHER *ROBBERY*.

S... SENSEI ...

MY MISSION AT THE MOMENT IS TO DEFEAT YOU.
COME!
GLARE
TM
WHAT ?!
ARE YOU RUNNING FROM MY CHALLENGE?
TM
TM
WAIT THERE FOR ONE HOUR.
THEN, I WILL TREAT YOU TO A *LIVING* HELL.

READ THIS WAY

T-T-T...
.....
HMPH...
THIS IS THE THIRD TIME.
MUST WE START AGAIN...?
HUH. THIS FEATHERED DOLL-MAN DOESN'T REALIZE WHAT HE'S GOTTEN HIMSELF INTO.

YOU'VE FINALLY MANAGED TO ANGER...
...THE MOST TERRIFYING MAN IN THE WORLD.

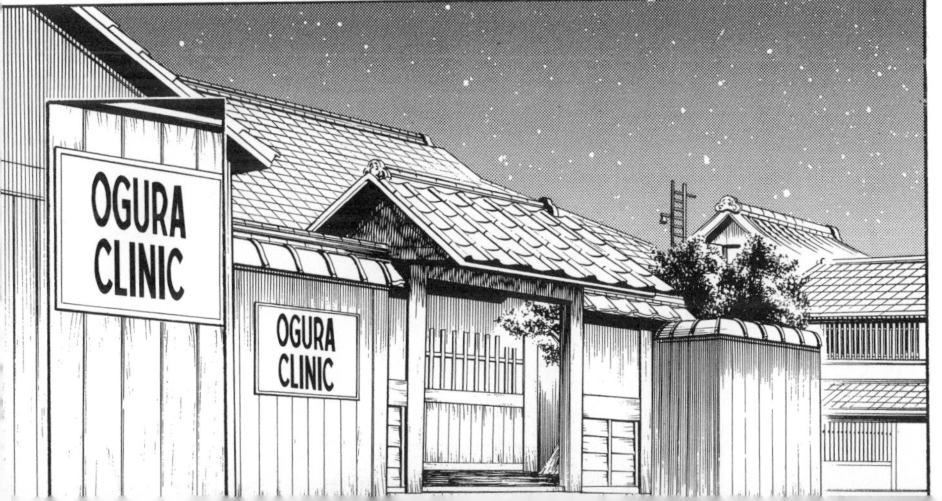

OGURA CLINIC
OGURA CLINIC

KCHK
≡PHEW≡
MEGUMI-SAN!
HOW IS YUTARŌ?
WHAT WAS HE CUT WITH?
THE WOUND IS GAPING, BUT THERE'S HARDLY ANY BLEEDING. I'VE NEVER SEEN ANYTHING LIKE IT.
I DON'T GET IT EITHER.
BUT HOW IS HE...?
YOU GOT TO HIM QUICKLY.
THERE'S NO THREAT TO HIS LIFE.
!

BUT...
BUT...?
THE NERVES HAVE BEEN COMPLETELY SEVERED.
THEY CAN'T BE REPAIRED.

IT'S UNFORTUNATE, BUT THAT BOY...

...WILL NEVER HOLD A SWORD AGAIN.

Rurouni Kenshin

Act 42
You've No Idea

ONE LUCKY THING...
THE SWORD GLANCED OFF KENSHIN *FIRST*. IF NOT, THE ENTIRE ARM MIGHT HAVE BEEN LOST.
HE'LL STILL BE ABLE TO PERFORM SIMPLE TASKS, BUT...

...NO...
THERE'S GOT TO BE A WAY!!

SWORDS ARE ALL HE CARES ABOUT!
HE'S GOOD AT THEM, TOO!!
THIS JUST CAN'T HAPPEN TO HIM!
YOU'RE A DOCTOR, AREN'T YOU?!
YOU'VE GOTTA DO SOMETHING!!

YAHIKO-KUN!

VMM!

T-T-T-T...

YAHIKO...

YOU GOING?
YES.
I CAN'T STOP YOU, BUT LET ME SAY ONE THING.
THIS "IZUNA," OR WHATEVER IT'S CALLED—

KAMA-ITACHI.

A PHENOMENON OF RAPID MOVEMENT.

CUTS WITH A VACUUM BETWEEN TWO LAYERS OF AIR.

!

YOU... ALREADY KNEW THIS...?

ONLY JUST NOW.

THE OPEN WOUND WITH LITTLE BLEEDING FITS.

IZUNA AND KAMAITACHI ARE BOTH NAMES FOR THE "SPIRIT OF THE WIND."

THE VANISHING OF THE BLADE IS LIKE A SUMMER MIRAGE...

...CAUSED BY AN INSTANTANEOUS DIFFERENCE IN THE DENSITY OF AIR.

THERE WERE CLUES...

...WHICH CAME TOO LATE TO BE CAUGHT IN TIME.

GG

NOW, AT LEAST, ONE'S OWN SWORD CAN BE USED...

...TO DESTROY THIS IZUNA!!

HE'S LATE.

IT'S BEEN WELL OVER AN HOUR.

HE WAS FRIGHTENED BY THE SECRET SWORD...

SHAH

...AND HE'S RUN AWAY.

IDIOT.
WHO RUNS FROM SOMEONE WHO'S OBVIOUSLY WEAKER THAN HIMSELF?
PWIK

OH. SORRY! I JUST MADE IT HARDER FOR YOU TO USE THAT AS AN EXCUSE TO RUN AWAY, DIDN'T I?
WELL, I WON'T STOP YOUR LEAVING. YOU'LL BE MUCH HAPPIER NOT FIGHTING KENSHIN.

IF YOU'VE GOT AN EXCUSE TO RUN, YOU SHOULD TAKE IT.
HEH
WATCH IT, YOUNG ONE.
I WON'T MIND PLAYING WITH *YOU*, TO PASS THE TIME.
I WOULDN'T MIND, EITHER. BUT ONLY IF YOU'RE SURE.
FOR YOU TO LOSE TO A STREET-BRAWLER, AND NOT A MASTER-SWORDSMAN ...
THAT *WOULD* HURT.
KRAK
KRAK

HYOOOOOO

THI THI THI
THI THI THI

TSK.

YOU AND I ARE BOTH OUTTA LUCK.
YOU LINGERED JUST LONG ENOUGH.

THE REAL THING IS HERE.

DM

RAIJUTA!!
I'M HERE TO AVENGE YUTARŌ!
GET READY!!
GYAH

KEN...
TIIIN...
BRR
SINCE WE'RE AVENGING THE SAME PERSON, IT'S BETTER TO WIN.
RIGHT?
...ALL RIGHT?
I'LL BE COUNTING ON YOU.
YES.

...AT LAST!!

I *WILL* DEFEAT YOU!!

GRRR

...

AND THEN...

...I'LL ESTABLISH THE *NEW ERA* OF SHINKO-RYŪ!!

KEEEEEN
NNN!!
HYOO
!
.....
DON'T BE SURPRISED.
WHAT KIND OF FIGHTER FALLS FOR THE SAME MOVE TWICE...?

READ THIS WAY

NO ONE CAN BLOCK THE *TOBI IZUNA*, SINCE ITS EDGE IS SO SHARP...
...BUT FOR A MAN WHO CAN TRACK THE PATH OF A BULLET FROM A GUN, *DODGING* IT IS EASY.

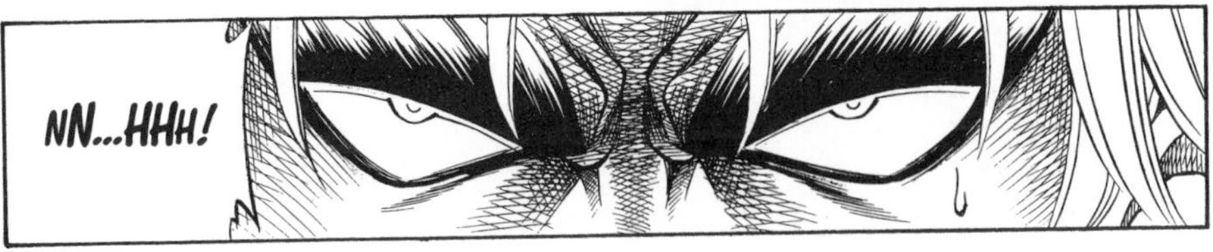
NN...HHH!

THEN HOW ABOUT *THIS?!*

NN !!!

NNYAAHH!!!
TOBI IZUNA...
...WITH RANDOM, MULTIPLE BLOWS!!

?!
HA HA HA!!!

NOW YOU KNOW THE *IZUNA*!!

TEN YEARS OF MY LIFE I GAVE TO MASTERING THIS TECHNIQUE FROM ANCIENT SCROLLS! AND *YOU* CANNOT BLOCK IT!!

THIS IS THE SYMBOL OF SHINKO-RYŪ!!

THIS IS THE ESSENCE OF *SATSUJIN-KEN*!!

HAPPY NOW?
HUH?
IF A LITTLE SCRATCH LIKE THIS THRILLS YOU SO MUCH...

...YOU'RE GOING TO LOVE THE *REAL* BLOOD.
ULP...
KENSHIN !!
—...
NOW IT'S CERTAIN, RAIJUTA.
WHAT IS?

!
FOR ALL YOUR TALK, YOU'VE NEVER KILLED ANYONE.
NO TRUE *HITOKIRI* WOULD BE SO HAPPY...
...ABOUT FAILING TO FINISH HIS OPPONENT.

YOU'VE NO IDEA...
...OF THE *TRUE HELL* BORNE BY AN ASSASSIN'S SWORD.

IN YOUR IGNORANCE YOU TOOK SWORDS AWAY FROM YUTARŌ FOREVER.

FOR THAT, YOU WILL PAY...

...AN EQUAL PRICE!!

Rurouni Kenshin

...NNN...
HYOOOOOOOOOOO
IT'S OVER. RAIJŪTA'S OUT OF HIS LEAGUE.
...KIND OF STRANGE, THOUGH, HUH?
WHAT IS?
GETTING CUT ON AN ARM THAT'S ALREADY HURT. THAT'S NOT LIKE KENSHIN.

Act 43–Settling the Score

COULD IT BE...?
HEY KENSHIN, IS YOUR RIGHT ARM—?
YEAH.

THE ANESTHETIC'S STILL IN EFFECT...
SO IT CAN'T BE CONTROLLED WELL.
HUH?
WHAT?
STILL, RAIJŪTA...
TP
...TO DEFEAT THE LIKES OF YOU...
...THE LEFT ARM IS QUITE ENOUGH.

Act 43
Settling the Score
伸宏
和月

WHAT ?!
FOOL !!
HYOOON

YOU'VE INSULTED ME ONCE TOO OFTEN!
YOU GIVE ME NO CHOICE NOW BUT TO KILL YOU!!
DOOOOOOOM
ZEEEN
FSH
NNN...

KEEEEN
KEEEN
NNH!!
FSH

MMM... IMPRESSIVE.

COMBINING MATOI IZUNA AND TOBI IZUNA.

HE USES THE *MATOI* INSIDE THE ZONE TO *PREVENT* ATTACKS...

...THEN THE *TOBI* FROM *OUTSIDE* FOR A FATAL SHOT.

THE IZUNA CAN'T BE BLOCKED, SO KENSHIN CAN ONLY KEEP DODGING.

HE CAN'T FIGHT IN HIS OWN ZONE.

LEFT-HANDED, KENSHIN CAN'T USE HIS *BATTŌJUTSU*... AND HIS *RYŪTSUISEN* IS ONLY HALF AS EFFECTIVE.

THIS COULD...

BE BAD.

ZSSSH

KENSHIN!!

IT'S HOPELESS.
FAST AS YOU ARE, YOU CAN'T MOVE WELL WITH AN INJURED LEG.
AGAIN ...
...DON'T GET SO HAPPY ABOUT A SCRATCH.
KEEP IT UP!
WHAT CAN YOU EVEN *DO*, AT THIS DISTANCE...?
ZAH
NOT UNLESS YOU CAN USE THE *TOBI IZUNA!*
PUI
THE *TOBI IZUNA* ...
IS, FOR THIS ONE, NOT POSSIBLE.
I WILL WIN THIS MATCH BECAUSE I CONTROL THE *ZONE!!*
DIE!!

BUT STILL IT'S POSSIBLE TO ATTACK FROM—
—OUTSIDE THE ZONE!
HITEN MITSURUGI-RYŪ!
BATTŌJUTSU !!
WHAT?!

HIRYŪSEN!!

?!
?!
PNG
.....

SHOOTING OUT THE SWORD FROM ITS SHEATH...
...LIKE AN ARROW— WITHOUT USING HIS RIGHT ARM.
GRIN...
HE REALLY DID GET HIM... WITH JUST HIS LEFT ARM.
KENSHIN!
TM

This happened a little while ago. In mid-April, I went to Aomori with J.S.A.T. ("Jump Super-Anime Tour"). It was a lot of fun, since I usually just stay put at my house. Meeting the fans was great, and seeing the sunset during the flight was really moving. When I stay at home too much, I start feeling cramped and start getting a negative mindset, as you may have noticed last volume. So, these days, I plan to take breaks when I need them, and work hard when I don't. See you next volume!

D... DON'T MOVE!

HUF HUF

MOVE, AND I'LL KILL THE BOY!!

HUF

.....

GG

KILL ME IF YOU CAN!!
HSST
LIKE I'M AFRAID TO DIE BY YOU?!
.....

HE SAYS DO IT.
WHY DON'T YOU?

YOU'RE ALWAYS TALKING ABOUT SATSUJIN-KEN.
SATSUJIN-KEN—THE "KILLING ART."
IT'S NOT ABOUT SCROLLS OR ANCIENT STYLES.
TP

IT'S ABOUT THE WEIGHT OF THE *LIVES* YOU'VE TAKEN, DRAGGING YOU DOWN TO HELL.

THAT...IS SATSUJIN-KEN.

IF YOU CAN'T UNDERSTAND THAT MUCH...

EVEN DEFEATING YAHIKO IS BEYOND YOU.

TUMP

N...

NYAAAH!

READ THIS WAY

NOW WHAT? SHOULD WE BREAK HIS ARM OR SOMETHING?
NO NEED FOR THAT.

HIS CONFIDENCE IS GONE.
HE'LL NEVER RECOVER AS A SWORDSMAN.

ALSO...
...IT WON'T HELP TO BRING BACK YUTARŌ'S RIGHT ARM.
......

HYOOOOOOOOOOOO

PWIK

... YOU'RE AWAKE.

ARE YOU ALL RIGHT?
TP
TP
MY RIGHT HAND... NOT MOVING...
SO IT WASN'T A DREAM.
I WAS BETRAYED...
...BY MY OWN MASTER...
YUTARŌ...
小国診療所

The Secret Life of Characters (16)

—Isurugi Raijūta—

He was supposed to be "intelligently macho and a believer of *satsujin-ken*," the opposite of Kenshin. Something, somehow, went wrong along the way, and he turned into a total fake. Becoming a smaller and smaller man as the chapters went on, he ended up defeated by a single blow—ending almost as a villain. Seriously, when I think back about this guy, I still wonder how it is he sank so low.

I guess the state of my exhausted mind and body can't help being reflected in the characters I create. But this particular guy taught me quite a bit, and I *would* like to give him some peace in future *RuroKen* stories. Then again...this guy—! Sigh.

Originally based on a character in a certain American superhero comic, Raijūta's looks started deteriorating as time went on, right along with his personality. In terms of his outfit, I'd had such a rough time keeping up with the complicated details of the "Oniwabanshū" storyline, I wanted to keep this one simple. Limiting myself to one design flourish only, I gave him black feathers...but then *those* turned out to be a major pain to draw, too. Every time I had to do it, I'd complain, "What moron designed this costume, anyway?!" Then again, he *did* teach me a lot about design...and macho characters *are* fun to draw.

Act 44
No Worries

TSUKAYAMA RESIDENCE
I'M VERY SORRY...
BUT THE YOUNG MASTER DOES NOT WISH TO SEE ANYONE.

THAT'S TOO BAD.
WELL, THIS IS FOR HIM.
THANK YOU.

WE'LL COME AGAIN SOON.

PLEASE DO SO.
BOW
THANK YOU AGAIN.

READ THIS WAY

I GUESS IT FIGURES HE'D LOCK HIMSELF UP.
BETRAYED BY THE MAN HE THOUGHT THE IDEAL MASTER...
NOW HE CAN'T EVEN HOLD A SWORD.

HE WAS MAKING SO MUCH PROGRESS AT OUR DOJO...
WHAT CAN WE DO FOR HIM?
I FEEL HELPLESS.
I CAN'T THINK OF ONE THING TO CONSOLE HIM.

...

TRYING TO SURVIVE THE SUDDEN CHANGES OF THE MEIJI REVOLUTION...

...I, A LOWER-CLASS SAMURAI WHO HAD NOTHING, BECAME A WEAPONS MERCHANT.

FOREIGNERS VALUED MY KNOWLEDGE OF SWORDS...
...AND I ACQUIRED MY CURRENT WEALTH.
WHILE THE FORTUNES OF MOST SAMURAI FELL...
MINE SEEMED ONLY TO RISE.

READ THIS WAY

BUT TO ME... IT IS A LIFE OF FAILURE.

EVEN IF IT WAS TO SUPPORT MY FAMILY AND KEEP OUR HOUSE...
STILL, EVERY DAY, I MUST LOWER MY HEAD AND WAG MY TAIL.

THAT'S WHY...
...I WANTED YUTARŌ TO BE STRONG.

LOSING IN NOTHING.
UNYIELDING EVEN TO TIME.
I WANTED HIM TO LIVE BY HIS OWN BELIEFS...

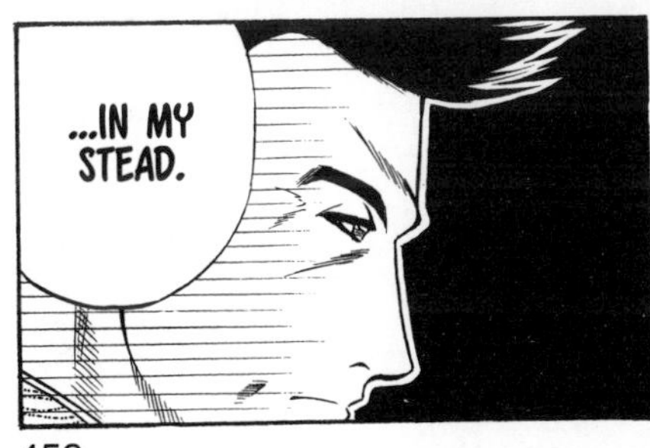
...IN MY STEAD.

A MAN MUST BE STRONG IN ANY SITUATION.
ISN'T THAT RIGHT?
...THIS ONE WOULD SAY YES.

IN THE END, BECAUSE I HAD SUCH THOUGHTS...
...I WAS EASILY DECEIVED BY ISURUGI RAIJŪTA'S SUPERFICIAL POWER.
AND YUTARŌ'S DREAM WAS DESTROYED.

...OH, THERE HE IS. KENSHIN—

ORO?
THAT WAS QUICK.

THE VISIT SEEMS OVER, YUZAEMON-DONO. THIS ONE MUST NOW TAKE HIS LEAVE...
...BUT WILL COME AGAIN SOON.

READ THIS WAY

THANK YOU. BUT THE NEXT TIME WILL PROBABLY BE THE LAST.
!

I'VE BEEN THINKING ABOUT THINGS.
AND I'VE DECIDED TO GO TO GERMANY WITH YUTARŌ.

GERMANY?!

GERMANY HAS THE MOST ADVANCED MEDICINE IN THE WORLD.
I'M THINKING, IF WE SEEK TREATMENT THERE, THEN SOMEDAY...
GERMANY
独逸
EUROPE
欧羅巴

AND...IF YUTARŌ LIVES IN A FOREIGN COUNTRY...
...HE MAY EVEN BE ABLE TO FORGET ABOUT SWORDS.

WE DEPART IN A WEEK.
WE DON'T KNOW WHEN WE'LL BE BACK.

AND THEN—

SHINBASHI STATION

THANK YOU VERY MUCH FOR EVERYTHING.

HEY, YUTARŌ. SAY YOUR GOODBYES.

I'VE THOUGHT FOR A WEEK, BUT...
...STILL I CAN'T FIND THE WORDS TO CONSOLE HIM.
YEAH. "HANG IN THERE"...
IT SURE DON'T SOUND LIKE MUCH.
....

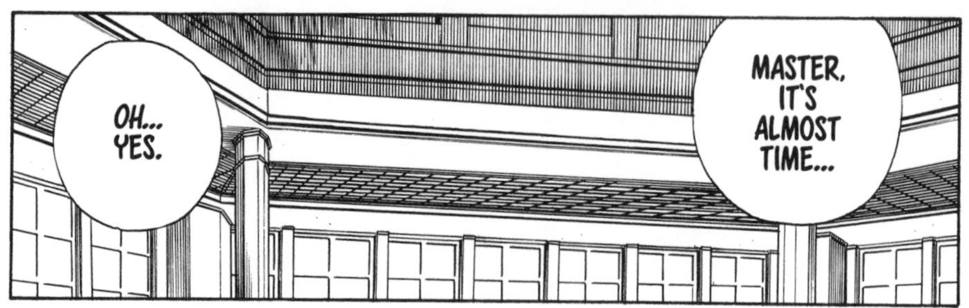
MASTER, IT'S ALMOST TIME...
OH... YES.

FARE-WELL.
TK
TK
TK

READ THIS WAY

TK

OH!

YUTARŌ!!

?!

?!
BAASH
YAHIKO?!
DM
WHAT'RE YOU GONNA DO?!
SULK YOUR ENTIRE STUPID LIFE??!

IF BEING BETRAYED BY RAIJŪTA WAS SO PAINFUL...

...THEN MAKE YOURSELF *BETTER* THAN HIM!!

I DON'T MEAN THE *REAL* RAIJŪTA, EITHER...

...BUT THE ONE YOU IDEALIZED...

THE ONE THAT YOU *THOUGHT* HE WAS!!

AND IF YOU SAY YOU CAN'T DO THAT...

THEN YOU REALLY *ARE* A LOSER!!

YOU...
GRR
YOU PUNK!
SAY WHATEVER YOU LIKE, BUT WHO ARE YOU...
TO CALL ME A LOSER?!
BAH
YUTARŌ!
I WILL NEVER QUIT THE SWORD!
WHY SHOULD I QUIT?!
EVEN IF MY RIGHT HAND'S NO GOOD, I'LL FIGHT WITH MY LEFT!
GISH
BOK
DOK
TOK
ALL I NEED IS MY LEFT HAND TO BEAT YOU, ANYWAY!
KOK

SO...

...YUP.

IT'S GOOD.

NO WORRIES HERE.

...NOW YOU LISTEN UP.

WE STILL HAVEN'T SETTLED THE SCORE.

新橋

SHINBASHI STATION

YOU'D BETTER COME BACK.

YOUR PLACE AS A STUDENT OF KAMIYA KASSHIN-RYŪ...
...WILL REMAIN OPEN FOR YOU.

SHOOOOOOOOOOOOO

MYŌJIN YAHIKO.

I'LL CLOBBER YOU FIRST THING WHEN I GET BACK.

KEN-SHIN ...?

THAT FARAWAY FACE...

ANYTHING WRONG?

NO...

JUST REMEMBERING WHAT MAEKAWA-DONO OF CHŪETSU-RYŪ SAID ABOUT THE FUTURE OF SWORDS.

!

WELL!

SINCE WE'VE COME ALL THE WAY TO SHINBASHI, LET'S GO EAT SOME WESTERN FOOD.

AND MAKE *ME* PAY AGAIN, RIGHT?

HE HAD SO LITTLE FAITH.

SO DID ISURUGI RAIJŪTA.

BUT WHEN I SAW THOSE TWO...

..."NO WORRIES HERE," WAS THE THOUGHT THAT CAME TO MIND.

...

HEH HEH

I AGREE.

神谷活心流

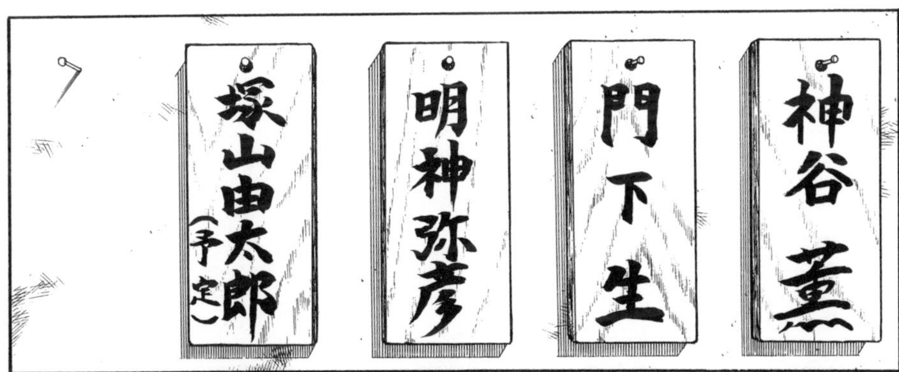

KAMIYA KAORU

STUDENTS

MYŌJIN YAHIKO

TSUKAYAMA YUTARŌ (RESERVED)

The Secret Life of Characters (17)

—Tsukayama Yutarō—

Created as a rival for Yahiko, there's no real model for him. Like Yahiko, Yutarō is a character who wants strength...but, unlike Yahiko, the origin of Yutarō's desire comes from a different place. In Yutarō's case, it's a "rebellion against a disgraceful father"—the complete opposite of where Yahiko's coming from.

Yutarō's admiration for an older woman (Kaoru), his admiration for Kenshin's strength, his recognition of their true qualities, these are some of the characteristics I imbued him with. Yet because they're his master's enemies, his inability to be honest about it—I developed these things as aspects of his youth. Overall, in my opinion, Yutarō is one of the good guys. Although, because he's been brought down a bit by my most disgraceful character (Raijūta), he may not have been developed to his full extent.

Whether or not Yutarō will make a comeback has yet to be decided. I have my ideas as to his mastering fencing and returning...but Watsuki also wants to have Yahiko, Tsubame, and Yutarō in this extra episode. Perhaps a story five years into Meiji, where the young girl and young men can shine... probably, though, it won't happen.

In terms of design, I've no real model for him either, but I drew whatever would be opposite of Yahiko—that's what I drew. I had trouble doing his hair at first, but once I got used to it, it was easy and I loved it. The image of Yutarō, though, contains no black...and, if I'm not careful, the whole page goes white. Compensating for that was kind of a pain.

Act 45
Extra: Sanosuke & Nishiki Paintings (1)

SAGARA
SANOSUKE
(19)
BORN FIRST SON OF A FARMER IN SHINSHŪ ON THE FIRST YEAR OF MAN'EN*.
RUNS AWAY FROM HOME TO JOIN THE SEKIHŌ ARMY AT AGE 9. REVERES SAGARA SŌZŌ AS A MASTER, BUT SŌZŌ IS EXECUTED AFTER BEING UNJUSTLY ACCUSED OF LEADING AN ILLEGITIMATE REVOLUTIONARY ARMY. THE SEKIHŌ ARMY CRUMBLES.
*1860
AFTER THAT, HE BECOMES A "FIGHT MERCHANT" UNDER THE NAME ZANZA, PASSING HIS DAYS IN MEANINGLESS COMBAT. HAVING LOST TO HIMURA KENSHIN IN HEATED BATTLE...
SANOSUKE BEGINS FREQUENTING THE KAMIYA DOJO. CURRENTLY LIVING A CAREER-FREE LIFE AT HIS OWN PACE.
赤べこ
NISHIKI PAINTINGS...?

YES. THE GALLERY'S FETCHING IN SOME NEW ONES...
BUT THE ARTIST IS SO POPULAR, THEY SELL RIGHT OUT.
AND WE CAN'T GET OUT OF WORK, SO...

...SO YOU WANT *ME* TO GO BUY THEM FOR YOU.
IF IT'S NOT TOO MUCH TROUBLE.

WELL... YOU *HAVE* TREATED ME TO A LOT OF MEALS, SO...
KLAK
FINE. I'LL GET YOUR PAINTINGS.
I PUT THOSE MEALS ON YOUR *TAB*.
IT'S NO TREAT.
KINDA ACADEMIC, ISN'T IT?
YOU KNOW I'LL NEVER PAY.

SO, WHICH PAINTINGS BY WHICH ARTIST?
THE SWORDSMAN IBA HACHIRŌ BY TSUKIOKA TSUNAN.

MM. "ONE-HANDED IBAHACHI," *EH?* EVERYBODY'S FAVORITE PRETTY-BOY SWORDSMAN OF THE BAKUMATSU.

BIG RISK TAKEN *THERE.*

HEE HEE.

UM... MM...

HM?

...

...OH... NOTHING.

IF YOU'VE SOMETHING TO SAY, LITTLE GIRL...

SPEAK UP.

...I DON'T. REALLY.

SIGH

ALL RIGHT.

I'M OFF TO GET THOSE TSUKIOKA TSUNAN PAINTINGS, THEN.

!

IS TWO ENOUGH?

MANHOOD THREATENED

IF I DIDN'T HAVE THIS JOB, IT'D BE *ME* THEY'D BE TALKING ABOUT!

NO FAIR!

DON'T GET ME WRONG, I LIKE THIS KINDER, GENTLER SANO...

BUT THE OLD SANO WAS... **WOW.**

"ZANZA," YOU MEAN!

HIS FACE WAS ALWAYS LAUGHING, BUT HIS *EYES* WERE NEVER HAPPY.

HE WAS LIKE A GRENADE, ABOUT TO *EXPLODE.*

COLORED, ENGRAVED PRINTS, "NISHIKI-E" ARE ALSO CALLED "EDO-E" OR "EDO PAINTINGS."

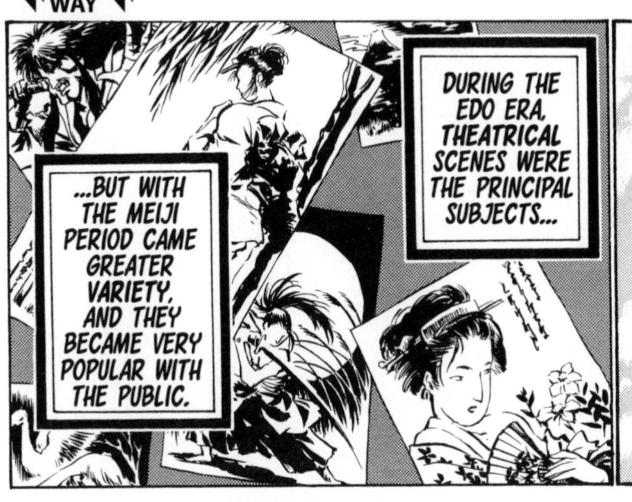

DURING THE EDO ERA, THEATRICAL SCENES WERE THE PRINCIPAL SUBJECTS...
...BUT WITH THE MEIJI PERIOD CAME GREATER VARIETY, AND THEY BECAME VERY POPULAR WITH THE PUBLIC.

TODAY, THEY SERVE AS GREAT SOURCES OF INSIGHT INTO DAY-TO-DAY MEIJI LIFE.

STEP ON UP.

HEY.

...SANO?

HEY, YOU TWO.
BUYING PAINTINGS? THAT'S A SURPRISE.

GIFT FOR A LADY, PERHAPS?
GRRR

SOMETHING... SPICY, MAYBE?
AIEE!
RRRR

I'M DOING A FAVOR FOR TAE AT AKABEKO... AND THAT'S ALL!
BO-O-ORING.
HOHO!
HEY GUY. YOU GOT TWO "IBAHACHIS" BY TSUKIOKA TSUNAN FOR ME...?
"IBAHACHI" BY TSUKIOKA TSUNAN...

YOU'RE IN LUCK— THESE ARE MY LAST TWO.
TSUKIOKA'S PAINTINGS SELL OUT VERY QUICKLY.

READ THIS WAY

TEN SEN FOR BOTH, PLEASE.
I SEEM T'BE OUTTA CASH. CAN YOU SPOT ME...?
ARGH!
SNAPP
HUH. THESE NISHIKI PAINTINGS SHOW ALL KINDS OF STUFF...
I'D NO IDEA.
THERE'S EVEN SOME FROM THE REVOLUTION.

SURE, THE ISHIN SHISHI PATRIOTS AND REVOLUTIONARY ARMY SELL ALMOST AS WELL AS SOUVENIRS FROM TOKYO.
IBAHACHI AND OTHERS OF THE BAKUFU ARMIES ARE POPULAR WITH THE PEOPLE OF EDO.

HST...
SANO?
...
THIS...

赤報隊一番隊
相楽総三
SEKIHŌ ARMY, FIRST UNIT SAGARA SŌZŌ.
月岡津南
TSUKIOKA TSUNAN
...CAPTAIN SAGARA!
OHH
!
OH, THAT?
THAT'S ONE SUBJECT OF TSUKIOKA'S THAT NEVER SELLS.

READ THIS WAY
BUT HE GOES ON PAINTING HIM...
...THE LEADER OF THE *FALSE* REVOLUTIONARY ARMY.

LOP!
..........!!
KUH
PEEK

...

WHERE... IS THIS GUY?

EH?

THIS TSUKIOKA GUY, WHERE IS HE?! TELL ME!!

GRAB

EEE...!

SANO !!

HE LIVES IN THE LONG HOUSES THE NEXT TOWN OVER! BUT HE DOESN'T LIKE PEOPLE, SO HE PROBABLY WON'T SEE—
HE WILL.
TM...
SANO...

NO WAY WILL HE NOT SEE ME.

......

TSUKIOKA

TAP

月岡

TSUKIOKA-SAN! TSUKIOKA-SAN!

TSUKIOKA-SAN! YOU IN THERE?

BAM BAM BAM BAM BAM BAM BAM

FORMER SEKIHŌ ARMY CADET TSUKIOKA—
—TSUKIOKA KATSUHIRO, ARE YOU THERE?!

...I KNEW IT.

YOU'RE THE ONE WHO PAINTED THIS.

SANOSUKE...

HOW DID YOU...?

I COULD TELL RIGHT OFF.
YOU STOOD BY THE CAPTAIN, TOO.

NO ONE ELSE...
HENH...
...WOULD PAINT THIS.
...YES. OF COURSE.
HO...
I SUPPOSE NOT.

I SEE...SO THE ARTIST TSUKIOKA TSUNAN IS *ALSO* A SURVIVOR OF THE SEKIHŌ ARMY...!
LET'S GO HOME, KAORU...
HE'S SANOSUKE'S FRIEND. SHOULDN'T WE SAY HELLO?
MM...

WE FOLLOWED HIM BECAUSE HE LOOKED UPSET—BUT THERE'S OBVIOUSLY NO PROBLEM.
悪
AND IT'S A POWERFUL MEMORY FOR SANO...AS HIS MARK OF "EVIL" ATTESTS.
IN THE WORLD OF OLD MEMORIES...
THERE'S NO ROOM FOR VISITORS.
HOW DID YOU SURVIVE?
I COULD ASK YOU THE SAME.

READ THIS WAY

...

...SO YOU BECAME AN ARTIST, EH?

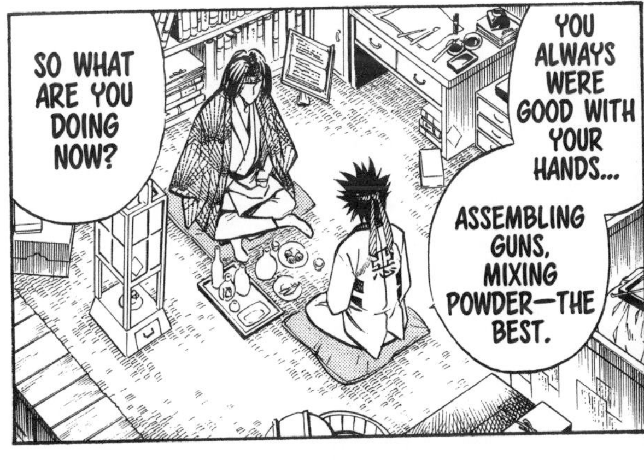

YOU ALWAYS WERE GOOD WITH YOUR HANDS...
ASSEMBLING GUNS, MIXING POWDER—THE BEST.
SO WHAT ARE YOU DOING NOW?

NOTHING. FREE-LOADING.
STILL...I'M PRETTY HAPPY TO BE DOING IT.

...
I SEE.
HAPPY, ARE YOU?
KOP
!
I HAVEN'T HAD ONE HAPPY MOMENT, NOT THESE PAST TEN YEARS.

I'VE SPENT A DECADE CURSING THOSE WHO FRAMED CAPTAIN SAGARA AND THE SEKIHŌ.
I DON'T RECALL LAUGHING EVEN *ONCE*— UNTIL I SAW YOU NOW.

YOU'RE EVEN MORE DEPRESSING *NOW* THAN YOU WERE *THEN*...
GLOOOM
STILL NO FRIENDS, I TAKE IT.
BUT, HEY...
...I KNOW WHAT YOU'RE FEELING.

TO MEET YOU AGAIN ON THE DAY I FINISHED PREPARING ...

PERHAPS THIS IS THE CAPTAIN'S WORK, FROM THE OTHER WORLD!

KATSU?

SANOSUKE— WILL YOU, ONCE MORE...

...FORM THE SEKIHŌ ARMY WITH ME?

WE'LL BRING DOWN THE ISHIN GOVERNMENT THAT FRAMED US...

...AND MAKE *REAL* THE NEW WORLD THAT CAPTAIN SAGARA ONLY **DREAMED OF!**

相楽総三

月岡津南

The Secret Life of Characters (18)

—Sekihara Tae—

To be frank, Watsuki created this character with almost no thought; she was just a plot convenience of the "Zanza" story arc (back during Sanosuke's first appearance) because I wanted Kaoru to patronize a restaurant run by a good friend. Personality-wise, she comes from Megumi in "Rurouni"...and then, next thing I know, she's the daughter of the owner of Akabeko, she's got the last name Sekihara, and, most recently, she picks up the habit of collecting Nishiki paintings. She's my first character to evolve this way, and I'd like her to keep evolving, surprising even the author himself.

As mentioned, Tae was created with no planning at all, meaning that there wasn't much planning put into her design, either. She's actually an update of an earlier, rejected model for Kenshin, with the "black" version of a Kenshin prototype hairstyle and a softer, female face. (There's no lipstick, to make the distinction between her and Megumi that much clearer.) The Akabeko uniform is tough to draw, so we changed her clothes, too. Purely as an aside, I originally set out to give Tae a Kansai accent and even went to the trouble of having it vetted by an assistant from the area, but it started getting kind of weird, so...pay it no mind.

Act 46
Extra: Sanosuke & Nishiki Paintings (2)

KATSU... WHAT ARE YOU PLANNING TO DO?

THE SEKIHŌ ARMY STILL STANDS FOR SOMETHING...

...THE CAPTAIN'S DREAM OF A *NEW WORLD OF EQUALITY* FOR THE FOUR CLASSES!

WE MUST CRUSH THE MEIJI GOVERNMENT!

READ THIS WAY

HAVE YOU BEEN SPENDING SO MUCH TIME PAINTING THAT YOU DON'T KNOW ABOUT THE SEINAN WAR?!

SAIGŌ TAKAMORI AND HIS FOLLOWERS—THOSE TOUGH SATSUMA MEN WHO WERE THE BEST WARRIORS OF THE REVOLUTION—THEY ONLY LASTED HALF A YEAR.

SAIGŌ RAISED HIS MEN IN KAGOSHIMA...
AT THE MOST REMOTE EDGE OF JAPAN. A WASTE.
MY TARGET IS THE VERY CENTER OF JAPAN.
IT'S HERE—IN TOKYO.
I WILL SHUT DOWN THE GOVERNMENT'S HEART—THE DEPARTMENT OF INTERNAL AFFAIRS.
IF I WERE GREEDY, I'D CRUSH THE ARMY, NAVY, AND THE MINISTRY OF FINANCE TOO. BUT I CAN'T DO THAT ALONE.
宗玄
酒
ALONE?!
HOW CAN I TRUST ANYONE EVER AGAIN?
I'VE DEVISED THIS PLAN ALONE.
SHP
STILL, EVEN ALONE, I HAVE THESE...
TUG
TAKE A LOOK.

I LEARNED ENOUGH ABOUT EXPLOSIVES WITH SEKIHŌ TO MAKE THESE.

THEY'RE GRENADES.

!

I'VE WORKED WITH CAUTION, TAKING TEN YEARS, IN ORDER TO LEAVE NO TRAIL.

ROLL

ROLL

NO ONE WOULD EVER IMAGINE THAT A MERE *ARTIST* WOULD MAKE SUCH THINGS.

IF WE DESTROY EACH DEPARTMENT'S HEADQUARTERS ONE BY ONE, BREAKING THEIR POWER...
...THE OPPRESSED FARMERS AND SAMURAI WILL RISE IN REVOLT THROUGHOUT THE COUNTRY!
THE GOVERNMENT, STILL WEAK FROM THE SEINAN WAR, WILL HAVE NO CHANCE.
IT WILL FALL... LIKE AN AVALANCHE.

THEN WE'LL BUILD A WORLD OF TRUE EQUALITY AND LIFT THE STAIN...

FROM THE NAME OF THE CAPTAIN AND THE SEKIHŌ.

I'VE ALREADY OBTAINED THE LAYOUT OF THE DEPARTMENT OF INTERNAL AFFAIRS. THE DATE IS TOMORROW...

A NEW MOON AND A SUNDAY NIGHT, WHEN THERE WILL BE FEW PEOPLE ABOUT.

...SANO, I WON'T FORCE YOU INTO THIS, IF YOU'RE LIVING HAPPILY THESE DAYS.

BUT I'LL DO THIS WITH OR WITHOUT YOU. AND, AS EX-SEKIHŌ, I HOPE YOU WILL JOIN ME.

GIVE ME A REPLY BEFORE NIGHTFALL TOMORROW.

...

TUK

TUK

...IT'S IMPOSSIBLE.

IT MAY HAVE BEEN WEAKENED BY THE SEINAN WAR, BUT THE GOVERNMENT'S NOT SO FRAIL THAT A FEW *BOMBS* AND *PETTY REVOLTS* WILL BRING IT DOWN.

IF HE DOES THIS, IT'LL END JUST LIKE THE JINPŪ UNION AND THE REVOLT OF HAGI-AKIZUKI.

HE'S BEEN SO LOST IN THE PAST THAT HE'S BLINDED HIMSELF...

...TO THE FLOW OF TIME.

TEN YEARS...

...HMF...

IT'S ALREADY SPRING...

...BUT SUCH A CHILL WIND BLOWS.

...COLD.

WHY AM I NOT SURPRISED YOU'RE NOT SURPRISED...?
NO, REALLY, WE'RE SURPRISED! *AREN'T* WE, KAORU?
WE SURE ARE, KENSHIN!
WHATEVER... LOOK, WE WANT TO CELEBRATE THE REUNION, BIG TIME.
CAN WE RENT THE DOJO TONIGHT?

OF COURSE, BUT...
...WHERE ARE YOU GONNA GET THE MONEY TO...?
GASP!
YOU'RE GONNA MOOCH OFF ME AGAIN, AREN'T YOU?! THEN THE ANSWER IS NO! NEVER!!
HEY, HEY...

DON'T WORRY.
I'LL TAKE CARE OF THE MONEY.

READ
THIS
WAY

OKAY? OKAY. THANKS.

OH YEAH, AND WOULD YOU TELL TAE AND THE LITTLE GIRL?
THEY'LL BE PLEASED.

WEIRD.

HE IS ACTING WEIRD!
SHAKE
IS HE SICK?!
WHAT IS THIS?!
ORO
...IT IS SPRING...
C-CALM DOWN...
SHAKE

...

酒
酒
...ALL RIGHT. LET'S GET THIS STARTED.

WHEN YOU SAID YOU'D "TAKE CARE OF THE MONEY," YOU MEANT YOU WERE GONNA MOOCH OFF *TSUNAN-SAN!*

SNORT

DON'T WORRY. LIKE THEY SAY...

"WHAT'S MINE IS MINE."

AND "WHAT'S YOURS IS ALSO MINE."

OR WAS IT...?

SANO...

WHO ARE YOU, GIAN?!*

...ANYWAY, WHO CARES?

JUST EAT AND DRINK TILL YOU COLLAPSE !!

*DORAEMON REFERENCE—ED.

GLUB GLUB GLUB
HAPPY DRUNKS ...
GLOP GLOP
BLARRRGH

READ THIS WAY

HYOOOOO
神谷活心流剣術道

ZZZZZ
ZZZZZ
KKHHHH
ORO
TWIK
TWIK
TWIK

AT LAST...

...SHALL WE GET GOING?

IT'S YOUR LAST DINNER.
DID YOU ENJOY IT TO THE FULLEST?
NOT REALLY.
THAT'S NOT WHY I HAD THE PARTY.

I'VE MADE AKABEKO AND THE LITTLE GIRL TREAT ME A LOT.
ROLL
ROLL
THIS WAS JUST A SMALL GIFT IN RETURN.

HOW 'BOUT YOU?

YOU HAVEN'T HAD A PARTY LIKE THAT FOR TEN YEARS. DID YOU ENJOY IT, EVEN A LITTLE?

NOT AT ALL.

HEH. GLOOMY, TO THE LAST.

...YOU SURE ABOUT THIS, SANOSUKE?

FOOL.

IF I'M NOT SURE OF IT, I DON'T DO IT.

AH.

YOU'VE RESTORED THE SEKIHŌ ARMY TO LIFE.
I THANK YOU FROM THE BOTTOM OF MY HEART.
LET'S HURRY. IF WE LINGER MUCH LONGER, THE SUN WILL RISE...
BEFORE WE CAN GET THE GRENADES TO INTERNAL AFFAIRS.
NAA
TWIK
TWIK
...SORRY, GUYS.
I WON'T ASK THAT YOU UNDERSTAND.
ZZZZZ

...BUT THE SEKIHŌ ARMY, IT MEANS...
TOO MUCH TO ME.

KENSHIN, WHEN NEXT WE MEET...
I'LL BE A GOOD AND PROPER OUTLAW.

I WON'T EVEN COMPLAIN...
PAK
...IF YOU BEAT ME DOWN WITH YOUR SAKABATŌ.

THREE HOURS LATER...

——.....

VPP

SHK

BLENDING INTO THE DARKNESS OF A NEW-MOON NIGHT...
...TWO MEN OF THE FORMER SEKIHŌ ARMY FIRST UNIT...
...MADE THEIR APPEARANCE BEFORE THE DEPARTMENT OF INTERNAL AFFAIRS...
...THE CORE OF THE MEIJI GOVERN-MENT.

The Secret Life of Characters (19)

—Tsukioka Tsunan—

The origin of Tsunan's creation was as a fake ad in the series, labeled "Mysterious Artist Appears."

Back when I decided to write extra chapters for Sanosuke, my sole concept for Tsunan was "comrade from Sekihō Army—lone explosive expert plotting overthrow of the government." But that alone didn't make him interesting, so I added the "fake artist" idea, and that became Tsukioka Tsunan.

This bonus chapter, like the Raijūta chapter, was written during a period of extreme exhaustion. On top of that, scheduling issues were created by starting the "Saitō Hajime" chapters as the colored launch of the magazine, obliging me to write the story over three chapters instead of within the planned four. So, to be fair, there are some parts I must confess never did get developed fully. As this Tsunan is the only character in the series thus far with a "mass media" connection, it's likely he'll come in handy later. Sure, he's a little depressing, but his straightforward personality pleases me, and so I'll probably haul him out again every now and then.

No model for his design. There really was no time to design anything at the time, so I tried instead to adapt an idea already in my sketchbook—a man in dreadlocks who, to my surprise, turned out to be just right (I'd thought that he might make a good villain someday). I made a few tweaks, and it all came together quickly. I'd wanted something "artist-y" for his clothing, so I added the bandana (don't start with me on whether or not there were bandanas back then) as well as the oddly patterned jacket.

Act 47
Extra: Sanosuke & Nishiki Paintings (3)

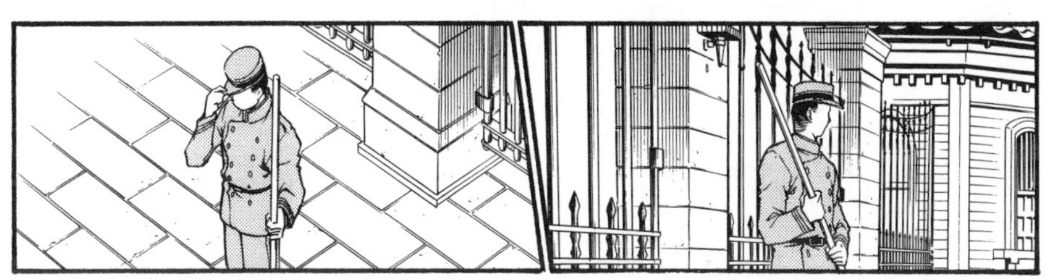

Act 47

Extra: Sanosuke & Nishiki Paintings (3)

WH- WHAT WAS THAT?!
A BOMB?!
DOOM DOOM
WAAH!!

MORE BLASTS! THERE MUST BE SEVERAL OF THEM HIDING!
DOOM DOOM
GET ALL THE GUARDS ON THE MAIN GATE!!

WAH
WICKS OF DIFFERENT LENGTHS ON EACH BOMB TO SPACE OUT THE TIMING, EH?
CLEVER.
WEEEE WAH
WAH
WAH
DDOM

IF WE CAN GET INSIDE THE BUILDING, IT'S GOOD AS DONE!!
INTERNAL AFFAIRS WILL BE CRIPPLED!!
DMDMDMDM
WE HAVE TO FINISH THE JOB BEFORE THE POLICE COME BACK!
GO STRAIGHT THROUGH THE YARD— NOT A MOMENT'S HESITATION!
TUM
WRL
GM
UP

READ THIS WAY

PANNNN

TAP

...I RE-MEMBER NOW...

GGG

THE CAPTAIN USED TO TELL US—BEFORE FORMING THE SEKIHŌ ARMY—HE WAS ORDERED TO COMMIT ACTS OF ARSON AND BURGLARY.
...HE MUST HAVE...

...
WHAT'S UP, KATSU? WHAT ARE YOU STARING AT...?

READ THIS WAY
BOOOOOOM
BOOOOOOM
KENSHIN...
HE MADE IT INTO THE BUILDING BEFORE US...
WHO IS THAT MAN...?
...
HIMURA BATTŌSAI.
THE MAN WHO WAS ONCE CALLED "HITOKIRI."

I SEE...
BM
THE LEGENDARY "HITOKIRI BATTŌSAI"...
DMMM
YOU'VE COME...
...TO TAKE SANOSUKE BACK?
NO.
THIS IS WHAT SANO CHOSE TO DO. THERE'S NOTHING TO BE SAID ABOUT IT.
THIS ONE HAS COME...
TO PREVENT THE *VILLAINY* YOU TWO ARE ABOUT TO COMMIT.
SWIP
...ISHIN SHISHI PATRIOTS, AGAIN.
DO YOU PLAN TO STAND IN OUR WAY?

...THIS TIME...

HYOOOOOOOOOO

...I WILL NOT LOSE!!

TOK
SSH
TOK
SSH
!
NNNN!
ISHIN SHISHI PATRIOT ...!

YES...AND BECAUSE OF THAT...

...YOUR STUPIDITY CANNOT GO UNANSWERED.

AND WHAT DO YOU, AN ASSASSIN...

...KNOW ABOUT ANYTHING?!

HYOHHH!!

WIP WIP WIP WIP WIP WIP WIP WIP...

HYOO HYOO HYOO HYOO HYOO HYOO

AARRR!

ENOUGH.

PAP

SHP

SANO-SUKE!

WE CAN'T BEAT HIM LIKE THIS.

BESIDES, WE'VE USED UP TOO MUCH TIME.

THE POLICE WILL BE HERE SOON.

WHOK

NNN

SA... NO...?

FORGIVE ME.

?!

READ THIS WAY

AND SORRY I HAD TO BOTHER YOU, KENSHIN.
...HEY.
IF I'D KEPT GOING WITH HIM...
WOULD YOU HAVE BEAT ME DOWN?
YES.
NO BAILING OUT ON FRIENDS.
AND NO MERCY, NOT EVER.

HEH...

THANK YOU.

...NN...
N...

!!
WSH
THIS IS...
...MY OWN ROOM.

?!

KENSHIN TOOK ALL THE GRENADES.
GONNA BURY THEM SOMEWHERE NO ONE CAN FIND THEM.

CURSE HIM! THAT GOVERNMENT DOG!!
GRRR

IT'S NOT LIKE THAT.

HE DOESN'T LIKE TODAY'S GOVERNMENT ANY MORE THAN WE DO. IN FACT...

...HE PROBABLY HATES IT *MORE*, BECAUSE HE HELPED *BUILD* IT.

DON'T TOY WITH ME! HOW CAN A HITOKIRI KNOW...?!
HE KNOWS.

HE MOVED IN THE SHADOWS OF THE MEIJI REVOLUTION. AS HITOKIRI, HE DID A LOT OF DIRTY DEEDS, STARTING WITH MURDER.
BECAUSE OF THAT...

...HE COULDN'T WATCH US DO THE SAME...

...NOT WITHOUT INTERVENING.

.....

KATSU. THE CAPTAIN TOLD US THE SEKIHŌ ARMY COM-MITTED BAD ACTS TOO...
...BUT HE *COULDN'T* HAVE *WANTED* TO DO THOSE THINGS.
赤報隊一番隊
相楽総三

THE ARMY LIVED BY THE IDEALS OF CLASSLESS EQUALITY.

WE CAN'T...
...DIS-GRACE THAT NOW.

...SO GLIB...

IT MAKES NO *DIFFERENCE* HOW DIRTY THE DEEDS!!
WE MUST USE *ANY MEANS POSSIBLE* TO REACH OUR GOAL!
...IS THAT SO?
KOP

THEN WE'LL *TRULY* BECOME...

...THE "FALSE REVOLUTIONARY ARMY."

DON'T SINK TO THE GOVERNMENT'S LEVEL.
SLOW AND STEADY IS FINE BY ME.
I'LL DO WHAT WILL MAKE THE CAPTAIN SMILE FROM THE OTHER WORLD.
KLA-TATT...
SHP

CAPTAIN...

...SO, HOW IS TSUKIOKA TSUNAN DOING THESE DAYS?

DUNNO.

ORO?

AFTER THE WAY WE PARTED...

I HAVEN'T BEEN ABLE TO BRING MYSELF TO SEE HIM.

GLOOM

OH! IT'S YOU, FROM THE OTHER DAY!

GET ON OVER HERE!

OH. YEAH. SORRY 'BOUT THAT.

WHAT'S UP?

TP TP

THERE'S SOMETHING TSUNAN-SAN WANTED ME TO GIVE YOU...

RUSTLE RUSTLE

READ THIS WAY

HE SAID IT'S HIS *FINAL* NISHIKI PAINTING.
...

I DON'T KNOW WHAT HE'S THINKING. HE SAYS HE'S STARTING A NEWSPAPER TO PUBLICIZE THE GOVERNMENT'S WRONGDOINGS.
I TOLD HIM HE'S ONLY GOING TO GET HIMSELF INTO TROUBLE ...
PFF

...SIGH... AND HE WAS SUCH A POPULAR ARTIST, TOO.

月岡津南
AH, WELL...
SORRY 'BOUT THAT TOO, OLD MAN.

TSUNAN'S LAST WORK?
GIVE IT!
I WANT IT, TOO...!
THIS ONE, YOU CAN'T HAVE.
TAE-SAN ...

—Crescent Moon in the Warring States—

As mentioned in the first volume, this was Watsuki's debut work, which therefore makes it quite nostalgic. It's set during the *Sengoku Jidai*, or "Era of Warring States," as the title indicates, but originally the story was supposed to be based in a fantasy world with Hiko as a knight and Isshinta as a farm-boy-turned-soldier, within a northern European milieu. At the time, I was seeing fantasy settings everywhere, though, so I switched to a historical Japanese period...never dreaming that the change would become permanent, much less that I'd begin an entire new series against a similar setting.

In this story, Isshinta is the main character. When I showed the first draft to the editor, he pointed to Hiko and said, "He's the main character, right?" I weakly replied "Uh...uh-huh," which shows you that I've been spineless from the start. What Watsuki had wanted to showcase in this work was not the strength of Hiko, or his romantic appeal, but the "kindness turns to courage" moment of Isshinta returning to the battlefield—teary eyes, drippy nose and all. It's typical in mainstream manga for someone strong like Hiko or Kenshin to dominate, but I've always been moved by weaker characters who grow into their courage. I've created many characters since, but this Isshinta, I feel, came out 100% the way I wanted him to.

End-of-Volume Special

Crescent Moon in the Warring States

SENGOKU JIDAI—"ERA OF WARRING STATES."

CHAOS REIGNS.

WHICH OF YOU CAN TAKE ME DOWN WITH HIS SWORD?!

THE BATTLEFIELD IS FILLED WITH MEN OF THE KITAKATA AND THE NAGUMO. MEN WITHOUT FEAR OF DEATH.

FLAP

NEXT!

FLAP

FLAP

WELL? DOES ANY MAN THINK HE'S STRONG ENOUGH?!

UOOOOH!

VNNNN

BUT...

HYAAAAH!

...THERE WERE EXCEPTIONS, OF COURSE.
AIEEE!
DDDDDDD

I CAN'T TAKE IT! I DON'T WANT TO DIE!
WILL I MAKE IT BACK TO THE VILLAGE ALIVE...?
DDDDDDD
NATSU—! ISSHINTA'S ON HIS WAY HOME NOW!
DDDDD
YOU!! IF YOU'RE A SOLDIER OF KITAKATA, FIGHT TO THE DEATH!!

戦国の三日月

IN EARLY WINTER OF THIS YEAR, THE LARGE NATION OF NAGUMO DECLARED WAR ON THE SMALLER KITAKATA.
THE SMALL NATION WOULD HAVE NO CHANCE IN OPEN WAR, SO IT SUED FOR PEACE.
NAGUMO'S LORD, IWANO HIROSAKI, RECEIVED THE BEAUTIFUL PRINCESS NATSU AS HIS WIFE AND A PEACE TREATY WAS FORGED.

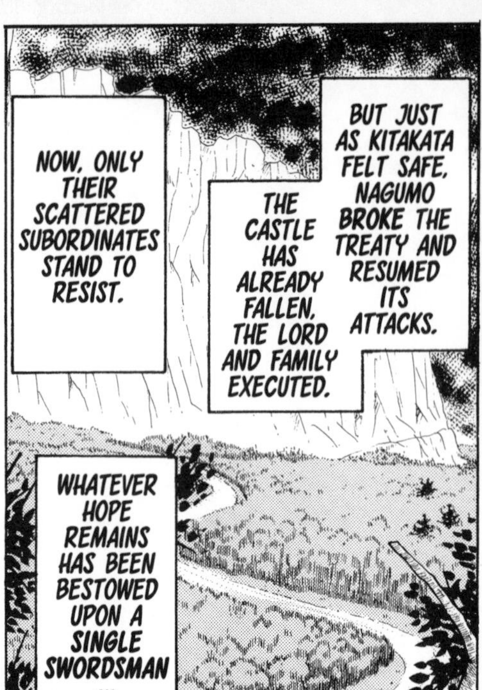
BUT JUST AS KITAKATA FELT SAFE, NAGUMO BROKE THE TREATY AND RESUMED ITS ATTACKS.
THE CASTLE HAS ALREADY FALLEN, THE LORD AND FAMILY EXECUTED.
NOW, ONLY THEIR SCATTERED SUBORDINATES STAND TO RESIST.
WHATEVER HOPE REMAINS HAS BEEN BESTOWED UPON A SINGLE SWORDSMAN ...

NATSU... DON'T GIVE UP!
HAH
HAH
I WILL COME BACK ALIVE!

GLP
BUT I'VE GOTTEN LOST... RUNNING FOR MY LIFE.
HAH
HAH
WHERE AM I?
HAH

YAAAH!
BMM

NK!
DM

NNH!

READ THIS WAY

HE'S A SOLDIER OF KITAKATA. A SCOUT?

UWAH

UWAH

WOBBLE

WHO CARES. KILL HIM!

I'LL SPLIT YOU IN HALF!

HELP!

GYAAH!

ZAAAASHH

?!

HMPH...

I MUST BE...

...AN ENEMY!!

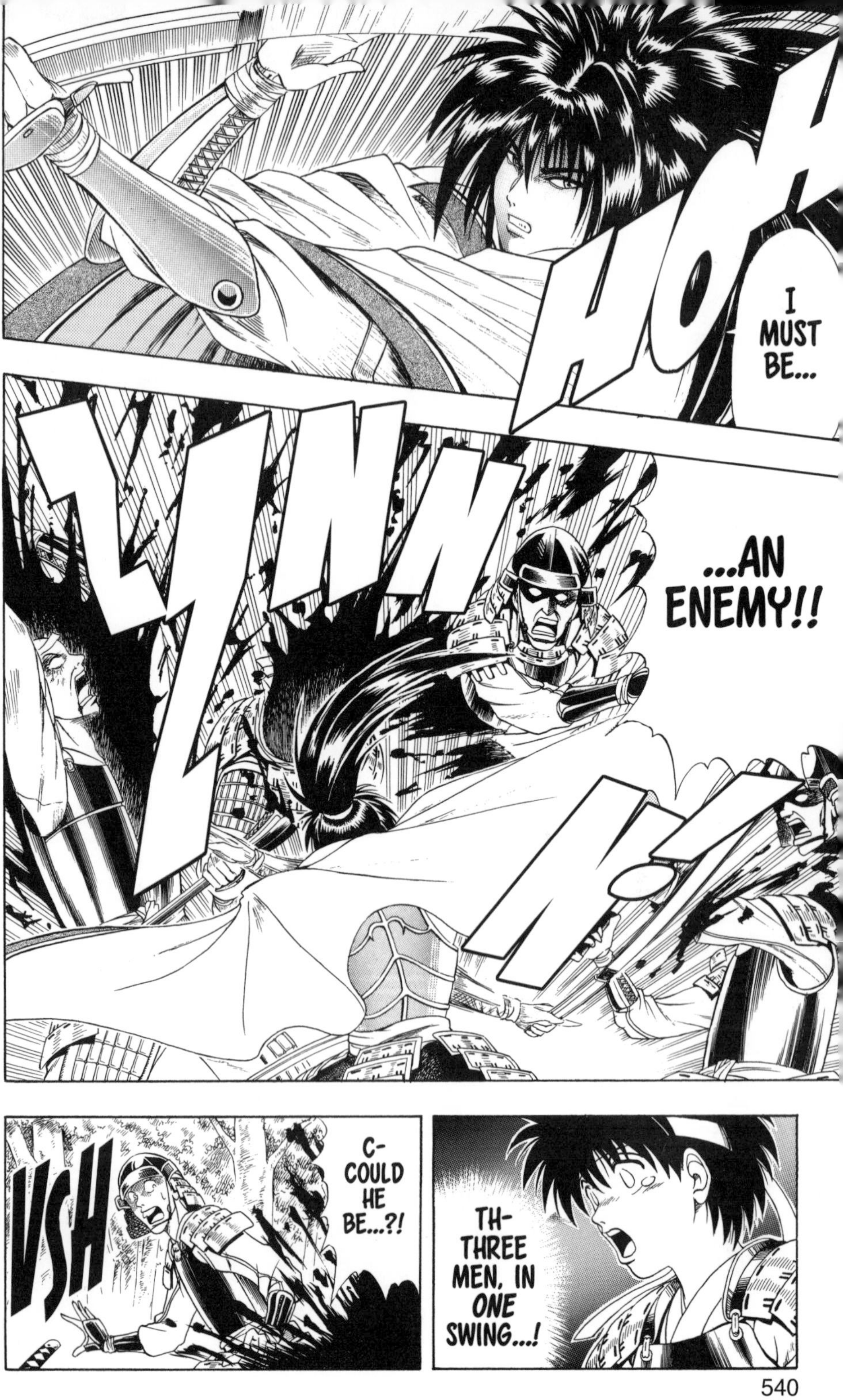

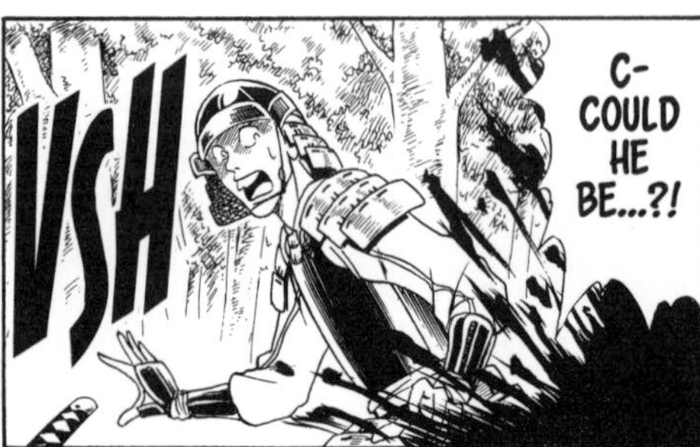

VSH
C-COULD HE BE...?!

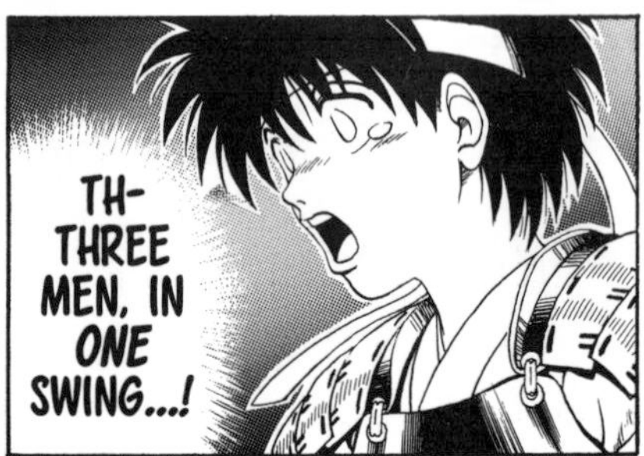

TH-THREE MEN, IN ONE SWING...!

READ THIS WAY

DN
NO RUNNING AWAY!

HIKO-SAMA!
HUGG

DOMP

THE LIGHTNING-FAST SWORD TAKING DOWN THREE MEN IN ONE SWING...!
MWUP
YOU MUST BE THE FAMOUS SWORDSMAN HIKO SEIJŪRŌ!

THE SAMURAI ALWAYS TELL ME THAT YOU WILL DEFEAT THE EVIL IWANO AND SAVE KITAKATA...
GRAB

B-TA-M
YOU STUPID FOOL! YOU LET ONE ESCAPE!

AND WHAT ARE YOU DOING IN ENEMY TERRITORY WITHOUT A WEAPON?!
ENEMY TERRI-TORY?!

OH... NO...

I FINALLY ESCAPED THE BATTLEGROUND... ONLY TO LAND HERE—!
WAHH

I SEE. A DESERTER.
A DISGRACE TO ALL SAMURAI!
VP

I'M NO SAMURAI—! I'M A FARMER—!

THEY TOOK ME FROM MY VILLAGE BECAUSE THEY DIDN'T HAVE ENOUGH SOLDIERS...
SOBB
SOBB

THERE THEY ARE! THEY'RE BOTH STILL HERE!
PWIK
KILL THEM!
VISH
HMPH. REINFORCEMENTS.
VISH

WAAAH!
FOOL, DON'T HANG ONTO *ME!* I CAN'T SWING MY SWORD!
I'M SCARED~~! HELP ME, HIKO-SAMA~~!

YOU'VE DISGRACED ME! I NEVER RUN!
DM
HE'S RUNNING! AFTER HIM!

NAGUMO HEAD-QUARTERS.

...WHAT?! HIKO SEIJŪRŌ HAS SURFACED?!

HRRRRR

GASP

INDEED, IWANO-SAMA! WHAT OTHER MAN COULD KILL THREE IN ONE SWING?!

GASP

GASP

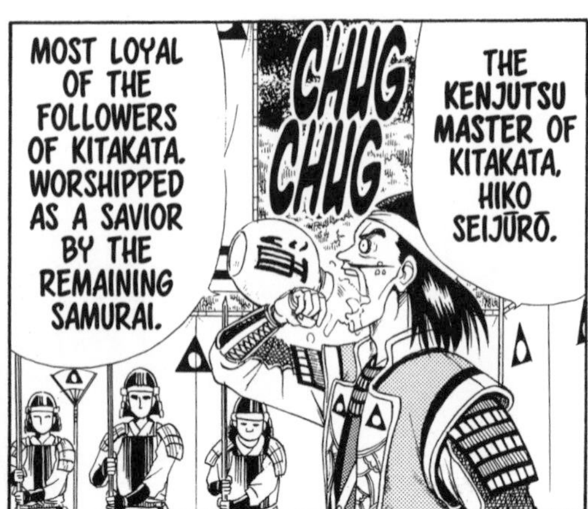
THE KENJUTSU MASTER OF KITAKATA, HIKO SEIJŪRŌ.
CHUG CHUG
MOST LOYAL OF THE FOLLOWERS OF KITAKATA. WORSHIPPED AS A SAVIOR BY THE REMAINING SAMURAI.

IN OTHER WORDS... KITAKATA'S LAST HOPE!
HE ACTS ALONE, SO WE'VE NEVER BEEN ABLE TO CAPTURE HIM...
KRASH

...BUT NOW IS OUR CHANCE!
WE'RE MOVING OUT! AND I'M GOING, TOO!
WHAT ?!
IWANO-SAMA, IT'S TOO DANGEROUS!

THE "HITEN MITSURUGI-RYŪ" HE WIELDS IS AN INVINCIBLE SWORD OF GODLY SPEED! WHEN HE USES HIS SECRET MOVES, HE'S SAID TO KILL NOT 3, BUT *100 MEN* AT A SWING!
TAKE HIM LIGHTLY AT PERIL OF YOUR *LIFE*...!

YES, YES, VERY IMPRESSIVE. BUT A SWORD IS A SWORD. HE WON'T STAND A CHANCE AGAINST YOU-KNOW-WHAT!
UH-HEE-HEE!

I WON'T BE SATISFIED IF I DON'T FINISH HIM MYSELF! LET'S GO!

IS HE THERE?!
NO, NOT THIS WAY...
TM
TM
TM
THEY CAN'T GET FAR IN THE DARKNESS OF THE NEW MOON! SEARCH THEM OUT, NO MATTER *WHAT* IT TAKES!
TCH...

THERE'S QUITE A NUMBER OF MEN AFTER US...
SNIFF
HOW DID I GET MYSELF INTO THIS...??
IT WAS SO *NICE* BEFORE. PEACEFUL AND PROSPER-OUS...
THE LORD WAS KIND TO THE PEASANTS, AND I WAS *HAPPY* TO BE A PEASANT!
WAAAH
BOY.

LEAVE BEHIND THE DAYS THAT CAN NEVER COME AGAIN. RUN IF YOU WANT TO LIVE.
THEY ARE DESPERATE TO SEIZE THIS OPPORTUNITY TO FINISH ME OFF.
IF YOU STAY WITH ME, YOU'LL DIE.

NO...
I CAN'T ESCAPE ALONE.

THEN YOU'VE CHOSEN THE GRAVE.
WHRR
NO!

I DON'T WANT TO DIE! NATSU'S *WAITING* FOR ME IN THE VILLAGE!

NATSU... IS WAITING...
NATSU! I DON'T *WANT* TO GO TO WAR...
I WON'T WIN ANY GLORY, AND I'M *SCARED*...
SOB
SOB

RRRRG! QUIT *CRYING!*
GONG

CRYING WON'T CHANGE ANYTHING!
YOU'LL *DIE* IF YOU'RE SUCH A COWARD, ISSHINTA!

GIVE ME YOUR ARM...
HH...

THIS IS A KEEPSAKE OF MY MOTHER'S—A *CHARM* THAT WILL MAKE COWARDS STRONGER. I'LL GIVE IT TO YOU SO YOU'LL STOP CRYING.

WHY DOES IT SAY "SAFE CHILDBIRTH," THOUGH...?
ARRG!
IT'S TO MAKE YOU *STRONGER*, OKAY?!

COME BACK ALIVE, ISSHINTA!
I'LL BE *WAIT-ING* FOR YOU!
I JUST *CAN'T* DIE!
I'VE GOT TO GET BACK FOR NATSU...!

...AH.
YOU RUN, THEN, FOR THE SAKE OF THE GIRL...
...NATSU.

YEAH ...
I'M A COWARD, SO THE ONLY WAY TO *LIVE* IS TO RUN...

...WELL, RUNNING WON'T BE MUCH GOOD DURING A NEW MOON.
IT'S PROBABLY BEST TO SLEEP QUIETLY TILL DAWN.

I KNEW I'D FIND YOU HERE...
LEAVING THE CASTLE SO LATE AT NIGHT.
EVERYONE IS WORRIED. LET'S RETURN TO THE CASTLE.
SEIJŪRŌ-SAMA...
WHAT FEELINGS DO YOU HAVE FOR ME...?
AM I MERELY THE PRINCESS OF THE LAND YOU SERVE, AS I AM TO ALL THE SAMURAI?
...
TO ME, YOU ARE LIKE THE MOON...
YOU SHINE A SOFT LIGHT ONTO THIS DARKNESS CALLED WAR...

TAKE ME...AND RUN AWAY FROM HERE...
I DO NOT WISH TO MARRY IWANO.
AS I WISH TO STAY BY *MASTER SEIJŪRŌ'S* SIDE.
IF IT WERE ALLOWED, I WOULD WISH FOR YOU TO STAY BY MY SIDE FOREVER.
BUT...
...THEN KITAKATA WILL BE...
BWM
?!
VSH
NGG
!
MY LEGS ...
PRINCESS NATSU!
NATSU-SAMA!
NATSU-SAMA!
NATSU-SAMA!

NATSU!!

WHAT?!

VWIP
N... NATSU...?
WHERE? WHERE IS SHE?!
VWIP

WHERE...

JUST A DREAM...
HFF
HFF
A DREAM...

READ THIS WAY

...YOU DON'T MEAN MY NATSU??
DO YOU LOVE... SOMEONE ...?

HFF
HFF

NATSU... NATSU...
OH!
OF COURSE!
THAT'S RIGHT!

THE PRINCESS OF KITAKATA TAKEN BY IWANO HIROSAKI IN THE FAKE PEACE TREATY!
GASSP
SHE HAS THE SAME NAME AS MY NATSU!

BUT... SHE'S A PRINCESS... AND YOU, HIKO-SAMA...
YOU DID JUST TEACH KENJUTSU... AT THE PALACE...

HMPH... YOU'RE NOT AS STUPID AS YOU LOOK.
IT IS AS YOU SURMISE. LOVE BETWEEN A PRINCESS AND A SWORDSMAN WOULD NEVER BE ALLOWED.

THEN...
...A SECRET LOVE.

BUT THAT'S ALL OVER.

I'VE NO RIGHT TO LOVE OR BE LOVED, NOT AFTER MY ABANDONMENT...

OF THE PRINCESS.

"ABANDON" ...?

IN WHAT WAY DID YOU...?
...

PRINCESS NATSU BEGGED ME TO TAKE HER AWAY THE NIGHT BEFORE SHE WENT TO IWANO.
BUT I COULD NOT DO THAT. MY LOYALTY TO THE LORD DIDN'T LET ME.

SO I ABANDONED PRINCESS NATSU...

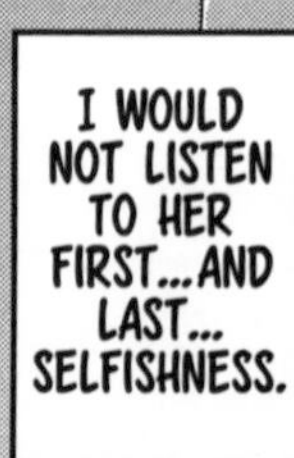

I WOULD NOT LISTEN TO HER FIRST...AND LAST... SELFISHNESS.

GNG
...NO. BEING LOYAL TO HIS MASTER IS A SAMURAI'S DUTY.
NO ONE CAN BLAME YOU FOR THAT...

BOOW
IT'S NOT YOURS OR THE PRINCESS'S FAULT! IT'S *IWANO* WHO'S THE VILLAIN!
HIKO-SAMA, I BEG YOU! DEFEAT IWANO!

UNLIKE ME, YOU'RE STRONG, HIKO-SAMA! YOU CAN DO IT!
PLEASE BRING BACK *PEACE* WITH THAT SWORD ONCE AGAIN...
AND PLEASE GO BRING BACK *PRINCESS NATSU*!!

IT WAS IWANO WHO TOOK HER... BUT IT WAS *I* WHO *ABANDONED* HER.

HIKO-SAMA...
AS DAYS GO BY, THE TEARS FALLEN FROM HER EYES CANNOT FLOW BACK...

ENOUGH. IT IS A FACT THAT I ABANDONED THE PRINCESS. NOTHING WILL CHANGE THAT.

PRINCESS NATSU...
PLOP
PLOP
WHAT WILL BECOME OF HER?!

YOU REALLY ...

I FOUND THEM! THEY'RE HERE—!

!!

BLAST!

READ THIS WAY

GUH

ZZZSSSHAAH

YAAH!

...

THIS IS BAD...

YAAH!

UWAH UWAH!

...

YAAH!

...

SHAKE

SHAKE

I DON'T WANT TO DIE...

YAAH!

SHAKE

PWEE

...

ALL RIGHT, ISSHINTA. YOU RUN ALONE FROM HERE.
WHA —?!

DON'T WORRY. I'LL KEEP THE SOLDIERS AT BAY.

AND...
KEEП
YOU CAN'T RUN WITHOUT A WEAPON.

THIS IS THE HITEN MITSURUGI-RYŪ HEIRLOOM, "WINTER-MOON."
ONCE YOU REACH SAFETY, SELL IT AND USE IT FOR TRAVELING MONEY.

THERE THEY ARE!!
YAAH
PWEE
NO RECKLESS ATTACKS!
YAAH
YAAH
SURROUND THEM!

HIKO-SAMA... MASTER, ARE YOU PLANNING TO DIE...?!

DON'T WORRY ABOUT ME! GO!

READ THIS WAY

BUT, HIKO-SAMA!

ISSHINTA, I DIDN'T COME TO THIS BATTLEFIELD TO FIGHT.
HUH ...?

I CAME TO FIND A PLACE TO *DIE*, AS SAMURAI.

I WILL NOT LIVE AS AN EMPTY SHELL. I WILL NOT LIVE WITHOUT NATSU.

WHAT ARE YOU STARING AT?
I'M TELLING YOU TO *RUN*.

YOU HAVE A PLACE TO GO HOME TO.
SOMEONE WAITS FOR YOU!

SOB

H... HIKO-SAMA...

ONE OF THEM IS RUNNING!

WSH

NEVER MIND THAT ONE! IT'S *HIKO* WE WANT!

I WAS GLAD TO MEET SOMEONE WHO CAN CRY FOR ANOTHER AT THE END, ISSHINTA...

HOHHH
I'VE GOT YOU!!
KEENG
?!
NNGG!
I MAY BE LOOKING FOR A PLACE TO DIE...
...BUT I WON'T LET YOU HAVE MY HEAD SO EASILY!
NOT MUCH CAN BE DONE WITH ONLY A SHORT SWORD, BUT STILL I WILL DANCE...
HYST
VSH
...THE LAST HITEN MITSU-RUGI!!

VNNNNN

TTTTT

HAF

HAF

RUN, ISSHINTA!

YOU, AT LEAST, CAN LIVE.

ZSSSSSSHH

READ THIS WAY

RETURN TO THE VILLAGE WHERE YOUR LOVE WAITS.

...AND MAKE HER HAPPY FOR PRINCESS NATSU.

HFF

TP

HFF

NATSU...
GNNG
NATSU...!

HF
HF
HYOOOOOOO

UHH...
H-HE'S A DEMON.

WHAT'S THE MATTER? CAN'T ANYONE FINISH ME?
I'M WEARY OF KILLING...
HFF
HFF

HIKO! A DUEL!!
HAAH!

READ THIS WAY

THAT VOICE...!
VP

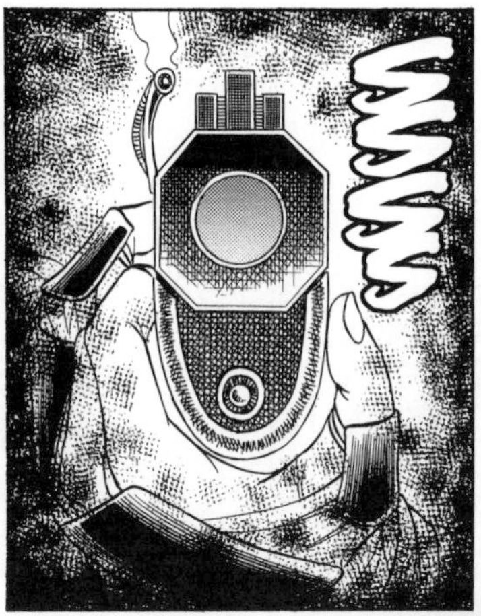

BOOM
GGH!

MINE AGAINST YOURS!
HYA HYA HYA HYA HYA
EVEN HITEN MITSURUGI CAN'T BEAT A GUN!

IWANO—YOU COWARD!
WSH

BOOOM

KKH!

YOU ARE KITAKATA'S LAST HOPE. AFTER I FINISH YOU, KITAKATA IS AS GOOD AS MINE!

FP

AND NATSU!

I SAVED THAT WOMAN FROM DEATH BY MAKING HER MY WIFE, BUT ALL SHE DOES IS *CRY*.

WSSH

SHE CRIES FOR *YOU!*

WELL, I'LL GIVE YOU TO HER! I'LL GIVE HER YOUR *BLOODY CORPSE!*

THEN SHE—AND KITAKATA—WILL BE MINE!

BOOOOOOOM

HUK

TP

READ THIS WAY

GODS...
THEN THIS IS IT... WITH MY MORTAL ENEMY BEFORE ME...
BLP
BLP

GLEEM...

THE MOON... THE CLOUDS HAVE CLEARED AND THE MOON IS SHINING.
THIS WILL MAKE ESCAPE EASIER FOR ISSHINTA...

BUT... TONIGHT IS A NEW MOON!
A NIGHT OF DARKNESS ...!
HSH

THEN THAT CRESCENT MOON...
IS IT...?!
OH!
OH!

YES! IT—

YAAAAAAAAAAAAAH!!
SHAKE
SHAKE
SHAKE
DHHHHHH
ISSHINTA!!

WAAAH!!

YOU IDIOT!!
WHY DID YOU COME BACK?! YOU MUST WANT TO DIE!!

I DON'T WANT TO DIE!
I WANT TO SEE NATSU ALIVE!

THEN TURN AROUND AND RUN!
BUT YOU, TOO!
YOU HAVE TO LIVE TO SEE YOUR NATSU!

...

I'M THE MAN WHO ABANDONED PRINCESS NATSU!
I HAVE NO PLACE TO RUN!
WAAH!
I HAVE NO RIGHT TO RETURN TO NATSU!!

YOU FOOL!
YOU CAME BACK TO TELL ME THAT?!
ARGH!

FORGET ABOUT ME AND RUN, ISSHINTA!
I DON'T WANT YOU TO MAKE YOUR NATSU CRY!

HIKO-SAMA, IT'S YOU WHO'S THE FOOL!
YAAAAA
DON'T YOU KNOW WHY PRINCESS NATSU CRIES...?!
AAAAA

I DON'T WANT MY NATSU TO CRY!!
BUT I CAN'T LET PRINCESS NATSU CRY, EITHER!!

DON'T RUN AWAY THROUGH DEATH, HIKO-SAMA!
IF YOU DO, PRINCESS NATSU'S TEARS WILL NEVER STOP!!
ISSHINTA...

SHUT UP, YOU WEAKLING!
BM
!
NATSU—!!
GLINT

BUAAHHH!
BMMM
HIKO-SAMA!!
ANSWER ME THIS, ISSHINTA...
TP
HUH...?

IF YOU RETURN TO THE VILLAGE, AND NATSU IS NOT THERE...
...WHAT WILL YOU DO?

I...
I...

I LOVE NATSU...
I'LL SEARCH FOR HER FOREVER !!
SOBB

OF COURSE YOU WOULD...
HEH...

NN?
WH
I'M TAKING NATSU BACK, IWANO!!
HSS

KEEP YAPPING. YOU CAN'T BEAT A GUN WITH A SWORD!!

CAN'T I?!

NOW LEARN THE SECRET MOVE—

HITEN
MUGEN-
ZAN!!

APOLOGIZE TO OUR LORD...IN HELL!

UWAH WAH —!
SCARY MAN!
PIDDLE
PIDDLE

READ
THIS
WAY

LAND OF NAGUMO. IWANO HIROSAKI'S CASTLE.

ENEMY ATTACKING !!
HH!

GAH!
THOO
!!

HFF
HFF

OHH...

SORRY TO BE LATE...
HFF
HFF
...PRINCESS NATSU.

HEE!
HAAH!
STUMBLE
STUMBLE
HIKO-SAMA, HAVE YOU FOUND THE~~?

HEE!
OH—!
HAAH!

AND DAYS...

...PASSED BY.

NATSU—! NATSU—!!

VNNN
WHAP

HYOOOO
......

WH- WHAT ARE YOU DOING?!
WHO ARE THOSE WOMEN ?!
SCREECH

CAMP FOLLOWERS FROM THE BATTLEFIELD, I SUPPOSE!!
YOWL
MORON! HE SAVED MY LIFE! AND THE OTHER ONE'S HIS WIFE!
YOWL
YOWL
"WOMEN" ...?

...WELL. IT SEEMS YOU TWO WILL GET ALONG JUST FINE.
WE'RE LEAVING NOW.
WHAT? DON'T YOU WANT TO HAVE SOME TEA?
ISSHINTA!
WEL- COME HOME!

WE HAVE TOO MUCH TO DO IN ORDER TO REBUILD THE NATION.
I'LL VISIT WHEN WE HAVE THE TIME.
WE'LL BE WAITING, HIKO- SAMA!!
!!
AND MORE PASS BY...

READ THIS WAY

"WOMEN," INDEED...
A HAIRCUT, MAYBE...?
...HEALING THE WOUNDS OF WAR...

REBUILD...? HIKO...? THAT HIKO...??
YUP. THE NEW LORD OF KITAKATA!
...AND BRINGING THE LONG-DESIRED WORLD OF PEACE.

OHHH~~! AND I WAS SO RUDE~~~!

AN ERA WHEN THE MOON SHINES GENTLY.

Crescent Moon in the Warring States

End

Glossary of the Restoration

A brief guide to select Japanese terms used in Rurouni Kenshin. *Note that, both here and within the story itself, all names are Japanese style—i.e., last or "family" name first, with personal or "given" name following.*

Hiten Mitsurugi-ryū
Kenshin's sword technique, used more for defense than offense. An "ancient style that pits one against many," it requires exceptional speed and agility to master.

hitokiri
An assassin. Famous swordsmen of the period were sometimes thus known to adopt "professional" names—Kawakami Gensai, for example, was also known as "Hitokiri Gensai."

Iba Hachirō
Famed historical swordsman (1843-1869) and subject of Tae's fancy

Ishin Shishi
Loyalist or pro-Imperialist patriots who fought to restore the Emperor to his ancient seat of power

Izuna
Raijūta's "secret sword" technique, a strike so rapid that it creates a vacuum in its wake

Jōdan, Chūdan (Seigan), Gedan, Hassō, Wakigamae
The five basic postures or stances of kendō. Jōdan: Sword lifted overhead. Chūdan (Seigan): Cut to the middle. Gedan: Low-level, downward/sweeping block. Hassō: Sword held vertically, hands shoulder-level. Wakigamae: Horizontal (guard) position. Kenshin uses Shinken, a variant of Seigan, against Han'nya, as noted correctly by Yahiko.

Kamiya Kasshin-ryū
Sword-arts, or kenjutsu, school established by Kaoru's father, who rejected the ethics of Satsujin-ken for Katsujin-ken

katana
Traditional Japanese longsword (curved, single-edge, worn cutting-edge up) of the samurai. Used primarily for slashing; can be wielded one- or two-handed.

Katsujin-ken
"Swords that give life"; the sword-arts style developed over ten years by Kaoru's father and founding principle of Kamiya Kasshin-ryū

Katsu Kaishū
Founder of the Japanese navy. Described famously as "the greatest man in Japan," Kastu Kaishū was born the only son of an impoverished petty samurai in Edo in January

Bakumatsu
Final, chaotic days of the Tokugawa regime

bokutō
Kendō weapon made of wood; also known as a *bokken*

Boshin War
Civil war of 1868-69 between the new government and the Tokugawa Bakufu. The anti-Bakufu, pro-Imperial side (the Imperial Army) won, easily defeating the Tokugawa supporters.

-chan
Honorific. Can be used either as a diminutive (e.g., with a small child—"Little Hanako or Kentarō"), or with those who are grown, to indicate affection ("My dear...").

Chūetsu-ryū
Sword style founded by Maekawa Miyauchi, sensei or "master" of the Maekawa Dojo, where Kaoru sometimes visits as a "guest instructor"

dojo
Martial arts training hall

-dono
Honorific. Even more respectful than –san; the effect in modern-day Japanese conversation would be along the lines of "Milord So-and-So." As used by Kenshin, it indicates both respect and humility.

Edo
Capital city of the Tokugawa Bakufu; renamed Tokyo ("Eastern Capital") after the Meiji Restoration

"goldfish turd"
Translated from the Japanese. A *kingyō no fun* is someone of little worth, a hanger-on, who profits from the skills/exploits of others by merely "trailing behind." In this story, it's the worst thing Yahiko can think of to call Yutarō, Raijūta's ostensible apprentice.

Himura Battōsai
Swordsman of legendary skill and former assassin (hitokiri) of the Ishin Shishi

Himura Kenshin
Kenshin's "real" name, revealed to Kaoru only at her urging

characters for "culture and enlightenment."

okashira
Literally, "the head"; i.e., leader, boss

onigiri
Usually filled with bits of fish or vegetable in the center, seaweed-wrapped "rice balls" have long been a (highly portable and convenient) staple of the Japanese diet

oniwabanshū
Elite group of onmitsu or "spies" of the Edo period, now known as "ninja" or "shinobi"

patriots
Another term for Ishin Shishi...and when used by Sano, not a flattering one

rurouni
Wanderer, vagabond

Saigō Takamori
Commander of an Imperial Army 50,000 strong, at one time Saigō Takamori was the most powerful man in Japan. Described as a "quintessential samurai who cherished the words 'Love mankind, revere heaven,'" Saigō would eventually become a leader of disgruntled samurai opposing the rapid modernization of Japan (on which they blamed the demise of their own class).

sakabatō
Reversed-edge sword (the dull edge on the side the sharp should be, and vice-versa); carried by Kenshin as a symbol of his resolution never to kill again

-san
Honorific. Carries the meaning of "Mr.," "Ms.," "Miss," etc., but used more extensively in Japanese than its English equivalent (note that even an enemy may be addressed as "-san").

Satsujin-ken
"Swords that give death"; a style of swordsmanship rejected by Kaoru's father

Sekihō Army
Military unit (formed mainly of civilians) who, believing in the cause of the Emperor's restoration to power, were eventually turned upon by those same pro-Imperialist forces and declared traitors

sen
Unit of Japanese currency, equal to one hundredth of one yen. No longer in circulation (no "coin" equivalent currently exists).

sensei
Teacher; master

1823, and would one day become the most powerful man in the Tokugawa Shōgunate.

Kawakami Gensai
Real-life, historical inspiration for the character of Himura Kenshin

Keiō
The name for the Japanese era that spanned the years 1865 to 1868.

kenjutsu
The art of fencing; sword arts; kendō

Kenshin-gumi
Literally, "group of Kenshin"—translated (rather playfully) for our purposes as "Team Kenshin"

Kiheitai
Fighting force which included men of both the merchant and peasant classes

kodachi
Medium-length sword, shorter than the katana but longer than the wakizashi. Its easy maneuverability also makes for higher defensive capabilities.

Kōgen Ittō-ryū
An actual historical swordsmanship style, Kōgen Ittō-ryū is said to be especially "spare" and is characterized by its economy of movement, with little extraneous motion. Used in this story by the bullying thief, Nagaoka Mikio.

-kun
Honorific. Used in the modern day among male students, or those who grew up together, but another usage—the one you're more likely to find in *Rurouni Kenshin*—is the "superior-to-inferior" form, intended as a way to emphasize a difference in status or rank, as well as to indicate familiarity or affection.

Kyoto
Home of the Emperor and imperial court from A.D. 794 until shortly after the Meiji Restoration in 1868

loyalists
Those who supported the return of the Emperor to power; Ishin Shishi

Matoi Izuna
Wrap-Around Rice Rope. Creates waves through the ground. Similar to Kenshin's Ryūtsuisen.

Meiji Restoration
1853-1868; culminated in the collapse of the Tokugawa Bakufu and the restoration of imperial rule. So called after Emperor Meiji, whose chosen name was written with the

Tokugawa Bakufu
Military feudal government that dominated Japan from 1603 to 1867

Tokugawa Yoshinobu
15th and last shōgun of Japan. His peaceful abdication in 1867 marked the end of the Bakufu and the beginning of the Meiji.

Tokyo
The renaming of "Edo" to "Tokyo" is a marker of the start of the Meiji Restoration.

wakizashi
Similar to the more familiar katana, but shorter (blade between 12 and 24 inches)

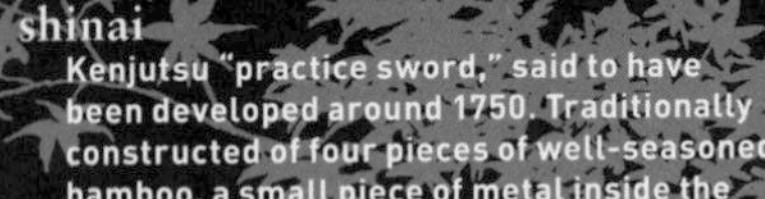

shinai
Kenjutsu "practice sword," said to have been developed around 1750. Traditionally constructed of four pieces of well-seasoned bamboo, a small piece of metal inside the "butt" of each stave keeps them aligned.

Shinko-ryū
"Old-school" swordsmanship as practiced by the revivalist Isurugi Raijūta. More a "league of swordsmen" than an actual school, the Izuna technique is its signature move.

shōgun
Feudal military ruler of Japan

shōgunate
See Tokugawa Bakufu

Toba Fushimi, Battle at
Battle near Kyoto between the forces of the new, imperial government and the fallen shōgunate. Ending with an imperial victory, it was the first battle of the Boshin War.

Tobi Izuna
Flying Rice Rope. Creates a traveling gap in the air. The sword tip shimmers like a summer heat wave.

The Bakumatsu

THE TOKUGAWA SHŌGUNATE

Rurouni Kenshin begins in the 11th year of the Meiji Era, but much of its story deals with the aftermath of the Bakumatsu, one of the most tumultuous periods in Japanese history. "Bakumatsu" means literally "the end of an era": specifically, the end of the Shōgunate. It consists of *Matsu*, "end," combined with *baku*, a prefix used to refer to the office of the Shōgun (such as the Japanese name for the Shōgun's government, *Bakufu*).

The Shōgun, the ruler of Japan at that time, was a military dictator. In theory, he was the Emperor's commander in chief, but in reality he ruled the country in an arrangement rather like that of modern-day Britain's. The Shōgun acted as a prime minister, handling the day-to-day governing of the nation, while the Emperor, like England's royal family, served a symbolic role. This system had existed in Japan since the 12th century, and at the time of the Bakumatsu the office of the Shōgun had been held by the Tokugawa family for more than 250 years. In the Bakumatsu, the Shōgun's supporters fought the growing movement to restore the Emperor as the active head of state but lost in the end.

ERA OF ISOLATION

The end of the Shōgunate also signaled the end of Japan's long-standing policy of isolation from other nations. It was during the Tokugawa Era (1603-1867) that Japan began its policy of isolation, denying entry to any and all foreigners. The country was also closed to overseas trade, with only a few rare exceptions allowed by treaty. (A limited number of Dutch representatives were permitted to drop anchor at certain approved ports, but that was about all.) This policy—specifically the restrictions on contact with Europeans—had been created partly in reaction to Christian missionaries who visited Japan in the 1600s. The Shōgun had suspected the missionaries of inciting revolt along with proselytizing the new religion, and as a result missionaries were driven away or killed. All travel either to or from Japan—native Japanese were also forbidden to leave—was banned.

However, Japan could enforce this policy only as long as it held the power to drive unwanted ships away from its shores, or defeat an attacking army once it landed. When United States Commodore Matthew Perry sailed his "Black Ships" into Japanese waters in 1853, demanding trade negotiations, the Tokugawa Shōgun, confronted with the fleet's overwhelming firepower, realized that the era of isolation was finally over.

WEAPONS OF WAR

Although the Japanese had long been aware of guns and explosives—a lightweight musket called a "harquebus," introduced to the country by Portuguese traders, had been used by samurai on the battlefield since the mid-16th century—there were very few items in the average samurai force that were a match for the latest Western weapons. The cannons of the Black Ships made that point clear. The Shōgun also had to consider China's humiliating defeat by Great Britain during the recent Opium War of 1839-42, and the distinct possibility of the same thing happening to Japan. Given the options of fighting a losing battle or negotiating, the Shōgun grudgingly agreed to a treaty with the United States in 1858. (Opium trade, however, was specifically prohibited by the treaty.)

THE OPPOSITION GATHERS

It proved to be an unpopular decision. Many powerful *daimyō* (warlords) disagreed with the terms of the treaty and wanted the Shōgun to go to war instead, not truly understanding the technological gap between Japan and the West. Other officials argued for a conciliatory approach and favored trading status for certain countries in order to buy Japan more time to modernize its own military forces. When British ships later bombarded the coastal city of Kagoshima with cannon fire in retaliation for the assassination of a British businessman in 1863, though, even the most strident opponents of foreign trade had to acknowledge that Japan was indeed militarily weak.

This realization did nothing, however, to discourage critics of the Shōgun, who blamed him and his government for the entire situation. They had a point: Japan's feudal system made fighting a modern war with a foreign enemy almost impossible. It had been official Shōgunate policy for years to keep the roads between settlements in bad repair, a measure designed to make travel difficult so that enemies of the Shōgun would have a hard time organizing revolts. Unfortunately, this also meant that Japan was virtually incapable of mobilizing a unified army against a foreign threat.

RESTORE THE EMPEROR!

Soon after the treaty, leading *daimyō* began to call for change, agitating for the restoration of Japan's ancestral emperor and a return to national strength. Pro-Imperial nationalists, the *Ishin Shishi*, took this argument to the streets but soon faced opposition from the *Shinsengumi*, a specially created pro-Shōgun strike force. The job of the Shinsengumi was to hunt down and destroy all enemies of the Shōgun. Before long, though, the Ishin Shishi had grown too numerous and powerful to be stamped out.

THE EMPEROR MEIJI

The situation came to a head in the year 1867: the Emperor Komei died and his 14-year-old son, Mutsuhito, ascended to the throne. The Shōgunate also changed hands, and Hitotsubashi Yoshinobu, who took the name "Tokugawa Keiki," came to power. Opposed by several powerful *damiyō* from the outlying areas of Japan (the first Tokugawa Shōgun had purposefully separated his enemies and reassigned them to far-flung regions of the country), the new Shōgun was defeated by pro-Imperial forces in the four-day Battle of Toba-Fushimi during the Boshin War the following year, and shortly thereafter, in a ceremony at Kyoto, resigned his office. The teenage emperor Mutsuhito renamed himself "Meiji," meaning "enlightened rule." The Meiji Era had begun.

MODERN TIMES

Under Emperor Meiji, a modernization program went into effect that would change every aspect of Japanese life drastically. In little more than 20 years, Japan transformed from a feudal, mostly agricultural society ruled by samurai with swords into a modern nation with a compulsory school program, a navy of steam-powered warships, and networks of telegraphs and railroads. The first Japanese-built steam warship, the *Chiyodagata*, was completed in 1863, and the Tokyo-Yokohama railway opened in 1872.

Modern Japanese business got its start during the Meiji era as well. Some of Japan's most powerful companies—*zaibatsu* (business conglomerates) such as Mitsubishi (shipping, manufacturing, electronics), Mitsui (the Mitsukoshi department stores), and Sumitomo (mining, manufacturing, banking)—were formed during this era as the new government pumped money into modernization efforts, paving the way for Japan's future "samurai" class of the 20th century: the salaryman. The Emperor moved the capital from Kyoto, where the Shōgun had ruled, to Edo, later to be renamed Tokyo.

THE END OF THE SAMURAI

Ironically, the era ushered in by the *Ishin Shishi* who had fought under the slogan *sonnō jōi!* ("revere the emperor, expel the barbarians!") rapidly became one of more foreign influence rather than less. Emperor Meiji met with foreign nations willing to recognize the new government, and even accepted advice on how to deal with those who had opposed him during the Bakumatsu. Many of these opponents were offered positions within the new government, while the rank-and-file samurai on both sides of the conflict found themselves out of a job.

The Meiji Era was a new beginning for Japan, but for the samurai who had fought to create this future, it was also an ending. Much like the gunslingers in America's old Wild West, Japan's samurai were obsolete once the process of modernization began. They were holdovers from an older time, outsiders in the new society their actions had helped to build. Like Himura Kenshin, the samurai who survived the Bakumatsu had to learn how to reconcile their violent pasts and adapt to a modern world of peace instead of one of constant war.

悪

Author Notes

Volume 4
Watsuki Lies for the Third Time!

I am so, so sorry. The promise made to you in Volume 2 has been forsaken. Watsuki is a bad, bad man (you may stone me if you wish). I should do as you see here and commit seppuku, but not before finishing *RuroKen* and not before finishing *Shin (New) Samurai Spirits*. Instead I'll suck it up, tighten the knot on my *hachimaki* and resolve to do my best. Please don't abandon me...Please...

Volume 5
A Year Already...Who'd Have Thunk It?!

Already it's been a year since *RuroKen* started initial publication in Japan. Just like the scene to the left illustrates, to me that's a real shocker! It's a tough thing, having a dream realized...but sustaining that dream after it has come true is even tougher—and that's what this year's taught me. It's been a case of dealing with chronic fatigue and a lack of manpower, but I'm gonna hang in there and do what I can.

Volume 6
Regrets.

In the previous volume, all I did was whine—that shames me to no end. I'm gonna pull myself together and do my best from here on in, promise. Changing the subject a bit, I've been thinking of buying a real samurai sword. It'll be expensive, sure, but I could...use it as reference material (yeahhh, that's it). And...I could be just like the illustration, and...aww, who am I kidding?! I do tend to lose it from time to time—especially when it *comes* to time—so maybe I'll pass on the real thing and buy a big-screen TV and enjoy *Shin (New) Samurai Spirits* instead.